Waves of Glory

Worship through Dance, Flags, Staff & Sound

Gerard Assey

Waves of Glory:
Worship through Dance, Flags, Staff & Sound

By

Gerard Assey

Published by:
Gerard Assey
19/18, Palli Arasan Street
Anna Nagar East
Chennai - 600 102

ISBN: 978-81-986974-1-7

Table of Contents

Disclaimer:

Any resemblance (names, characters, and scenarios used in this book, including testimonies and personal stories) to actual persons, living or dead, or actual events is purely coincidental. These examples are used solely for illustrative and teaching purposes.

The intent is to inspire and equip readers, not to depict real individuals or specific events. No harm or misrepresentation is intended.

Author's Heart Behind This Book

Hosting Heaven Through Movement, Sound & Sacred Expression

I never imagined I would write this book. In fact, had you asked me years ago whether dance, flags, staffs, or the sound of the shofar could have a place in worship outside of children's ministry or cultural tradition, I may have politely nodded, but dismissed it as something "other churches" do.

But God, in His mercy, began to open my eyes.

It started not in a crowded service or a grand conference, but in the stillness of a personal worship moment—alone in my living room. I remember standing, hands lifted, as soft worship music played. Suddenly, I felt a prompting—not in my mind, but in my spirit—to move. Just a step forward. Then a turn. Then my arms raised not just in surrender, but in declaration. What began as obedience quickly became encounter. The room felt charged, not with emotion, but with Presence. It was as if heaven leaned in. I had moved… and God had moved closer.

From that moment on, I couldn't go back to stillness. Not because movement is superior, but because I had tasted something real—an invitation to worship with my whole being, not just my voice or intellect. And I believe, now more than ever, that God is restoring the tabernacle of David (Amos 9:11)—a worship marked by expressive sound, sacred movement, and prophetic release.

This book is not for performers. It is not for perfectionists. It is not even just for artists.

This book is for the hungry.

- ✓ For the mother who dances in her kitchen when no one is watching.
- ✓ For the young man who hesitates to wave a flag, fearing judgment.
- ✓ For the older saint who hears the shofar and feels something stir inside, though they can't explain it.
- ✓ For the worship leader, the intercessor, the quiet-hearted worshipper who senses that God is inviting His people to go deeper—not just in theology, but in tangible, visible expression.

We are made in the image of the Creator. We were born to create, move, declare, release sound, and respond to His glory with everything we are. The Psalms are full of commands—not just suggestions—to shout, dance, clap, play instruments, and lift banners. These are not ancient cultural practices to be archived, but divine patterns to be revived.

Throughout this book, I have woven biblical truths, spiritual insights, and fictional—but very real-feeling—stories of ordinary people encountering an extraordinary God through expressive worship. Their names may not be found in Scripture, but their journeys are inspired by the living Word.

You'll meet people like Liyana, a quiet woman who discovered her voice through prophetic dance... Aadya, a teenager who waved a flag and watched generational curses break... Reuben, a father who reclaimed his identity in worship with a staff... and Eli and Priya, a couple who led a small, tired church into a revival of movement and sound that turned their town upside down.

These aren't heroes. They are worshippers.

And so are you.
If at any point you feel unqualified or awkward reading this, good. That means you're precisely the kind of person God loves to move through.
My prayer is that this book doesn't just fill your head with ideas, but sets your spirit on fire with divine permission—to move, to dance, to lift, to declare, to release heaven through your body, sound, and presence.
This is more than a book. It's a call to arms—and to feet, flags, staffs, shofars, and sacred creativity.
Let everything that has breath praise the Lord.
Let every movement glorify His name.
Let every sound resound with His glory.
He is worthy—not just of our words, but of our whole worship.

With joy and dancing,
Gerard Assey
Servant | Songwriter | Worship Coach
The Travelling Worship School
Advancing His Kingdom…through sound and sacred expression.

Introduction:
The Awakening of Creative Worship

There is a sound rising—a movement, not of words alone, but of heart, body, and spirit converging in radical surrender to the glory of God. Across nations, cultures, and generations, there is a stirring in the hearts of believers who are seeking to worship God not just with their voices, but with their *entire being*. They are dancers in secret, flag-bearers in prayer closets, and shofar blowers in silent valleys. They are the ones being called into a deeper expression of divine intimacy—one that goes beyond traditional forms and enters the realms of prophetic worship.
This book is written for them.

Rediscovering the Depths of Worship Beyond Words

For too long, worship has been narrowly defined as singing songs before a sermon. While singing is certainly part of worship, it is far from its totality. Worship, at its essence, is a response to the revelation of God—and such a response cannot be limited to vocal cords alone. Worship was never meant to be restricted to pews or stages; it was meant to be *embodied*—poured out through movement, color, sound, and creative expression.

In the Scriptures, we see this clearly. When the children of Israel crossed the Red Sea and their deliverance became undeniable, Miriam the prophetess took a tambourine in her hand, and all the women followed her, dancing and singing praises (Exodus 15:20-21). When the Ark of the Covenant was brought into Jerusalem, David danced before the Lord with all his might, shedding the royal dignity of his robe in favor of the raw abandon of worship (2 Samuel 6:14). These were not rehearsed or restrained acts—they were visceral, powerful, and sacred expressions of awe, joy, and reverence.

In the New Testament, while the forms of worship evolved with the spreading gospel, the freedom of expression remained. Paul and Silas, in a prison cell, sang hymns and prayed aloud until the earth shook (Acts 16:25-26)—worship, once again, was not just verbal; it carried a spiritual authority that transcended physical chains.

Worship that moves heaven often moves the body first. And yet, many in today's church have been conditioned to view expressive worship as emotionalism or distraction. This book challenges that mindset and calls us to *return to the biblical roots of holistic worship.*

God's Desire for Whole-Being Worship

In Mark 12:30, Jesus declares the greatest commandment: *"Love the Lord your God with all your heart and with all your soul and with all your mind and with all your strength."* This is the full engagement of the human being. And worship is, in essence, the overflow of love.

God designed worship not only to be *heard*, but also *seen*. The Hebrew word for worship, "shachah," literally means *"to bow down or prostrate oneself."* It is physical. Similarly, other Hebrew expressions—"halal" (to boast, rave), "zamar" (to play instruments), "tehillah" (to sing aloud), "machowl" (to dance)—all point to a dynamic, expressive, and embodied form of worship.

This reveals God's deep desire: not just for our words, but for our *whole person*—spirit, soul, and body—to glorify Him.
Let us imagine a fictional story that reflects this truth.

The Story of Deborah – A Journey of Redeemed Expression

Deborah was a schoolteacher in her early forties, soft-spoken and deeply committed to God. She was known in her church as a faithful intercessor, but never one to draw attention. As a child, Deborah had loved to dance. But a critical remark from a relative during her teen years—"That's not what good Christian girls do"—shut her passion down. For decades, she believed that expressive movement was worldly, inappropriate, even shameful.

That was until a conference she reluctantly attended, where the worship team used flags during a song. Deborah watched as the colors swirled in the air—crimson, gold, blue—like heaven had descended into the sanctuary. As the dancers moved with grace, she felt something stir. Tears began to flow. Something deep, dormant, and holy was waking up.

Over the months that followed, she began dancing in her living room again. First timidly, then with boldness. She bought a simple white flag and began waving it in her prayer time. She didn't understand everything at first, but she knew one thing: her worship had grown deeper. Her body was no longer a bystander; it had become an *instrument of praise*.

Years later, she started a ministry to teach women how to worship through movement. *"Worship isn't just what we say,"* she often told them, *"It's what we surrender—and my body is now surrendered."*

Why This Book and Why Now?

The world is becoming increasingly visual, expressive, and creative—and the Church must not lag behind in engaging the full spectrum of God-given expression in worship. We are in a season where God is restoring the Tabernacle of David—a place where worship was constant, vibrant, and extravagant (Amos 9:11). This restoration includes banners raised in His name, dancers moving prophetically, staff bearers symbolizing spiritual authority, and shofars releasing divine decrees into the atmosphere.

The enemy has always sought to suppress creative worship, because he knows that *movement in worship carries breakthrough power.* If he can keep us passive, he can keep us bound. But when worshipers rise with their instruments—whether flag, staff, voice, or dance—the heavens respond.

This book comes as both a call and a guide: a call to return to the full-bodied worship God designed, and a guide to help you walk into it—with understanding, reverence, and joy. Whether you are a curious believer, a worship leader, or a seasoned intercessor, there is something in this book for you.

May this journey lead you into deeper intimacy with the Lord, where every wave of your worship releases His glory.

Reflective Action Plan:

- ✓ Ask God to reveal if there are areas in your life where you've restricted your worship to only words or songs. Invite Him to teach you what it means to worship with your whole being.
- ✓ Try expressing worship physically in a private setting: dance, wave a scarf, or move your

arms during prayer. Notice how it feels to surrender your body in praise.

- ✓ Write a journal entry reflecting on the following:
"Lord, are there parts of me I have withheld from You in worship? Teach me to surrender not only my voice but my body, my emotions, and my movements to You."

PART 1:
FOUNDATIONS OF EXPRESSIVE WORSHIP

Chapter 1:
What is Worship?

Worship is not a genre. It is not a segment in a church service. It is not an emotional moment orchestrated by the right blend of voices and instruments. Worship is deeper than any sound, longer than any song, and broader than any style. True worship is a lifestyle—an ongoing, daily response to the worthiness of God.

Many today equate worship with singing. And while music is a powerful medium through which worship is expressed, worship itself is far more than melody. Worship is not performance. It is surrender. It is not entertainment. It is exaltation. Worship is the divine rhythm of heaven echoing through human lives that have laid themselves down in love.

Worship as a Lifestyle, Not a Performance

The apostle Paul writes in Romans 12:1, *"Therefore, I urge you, brothers and sisters, in view of God's mercy, to offer your bodies as a living sacrifice, holy and pleasing to God—this is your true and proper worship."*

This verse is one of the most foundational descriptions of worship in the Bible. It has nothing to do with singing. Paul describes worship as the offering of our *bodies*—our entire beings—as *living sacrifices*. In the Old Testament, worship often involved physical offerings—lambs, grain, incense. But under the new covenant, God desires something far more intimate: He wants us. Our thoughts, actions, motives, decisions, movement—all surrendered to Him.

This perspective was foreign to Marcus, a successful marketing executive from Johannesburg who had recently rededicated his life to Christ. Raised in a traditional church where worship was formal and highly structured, Marcus had always believed that worship was something that belonged to the choir. He loved music, but he never considered himself a "worshipper."

Everything changed after a business trip brought him to a small church service in a rural town. There, he watched as men and women worshipped freely—some lifting their hands, others dancing softly, one elderly woman quietly weeping as she waved a simple white scarf in the air. It was not showy or polished. But it was *real*. For the first time in his life, Marcus realized worship had nothing to do with skill. It had everything to do with surrender. That night, alone in his hotel room, Marcus knelt beside his bed and said, "God, I give You not just my voice, but my life. Teach me to live worship." And from that day, the boardroom became a sanctuary. Every pitch, every decision, every client interaction—an opportunity to glorify the One who saved him.

Biblical Foundations of Worship

In John 4, Jesus meets a Samaritan woman at a well and reveals one of the most profound truths about worship in the entire New Testament.

"Yet a time is coming and has now come when the true worshipers will worship the Father in the Spirit and in truth, for they are the kind of worshipers the Father seeks. God is spirit, and his worshipers must worship in the Spirit and in truth." – John 4:23–24

This exchange takes place with a woman whose life was riddled with brokenness, shame, and religious confusion. She wanted to argue about the correct place to worship—Mount Gerizim or Jerusalem. But Jesus shifts the conversation away from *location* and toward *condition*. He reveals that worship is not about where, but how—and more importantly, who.

To worship in spirit is to worship with your innermost being—authentically, passionately, and led by the Holy Spirit. To worship in truth is to worship in alignment with the Word of God, without pretense or hypocrisy. This kind of worship is what the Father seeks—not simply receives, but *pursues*.

The Greek word used here for "worship" is proskuneo, which literally means "to kiss toward" or "to bow down in reverence." It denotes intimacy and submission. In Hebrew, a similar word is shachah, meaning "to prostrate oneself, to fall down in homage." These ancient words paint a picture of worship as deeply relational and reverent—not casual or half-hearted, but sacred and wholehearted.

Hebrew & Greek Words that Reveal Worship's Depth

The Bible is filled with vibrant language that unveils the multifaceted nature of worship. In Hebrew, we encounter a spectrum of terms:

- ✓ Shachah *(Strong's H7812): To bow down, prostrate oneself in reverence.*
- ✓ Halal *(H1984): To shine, boast, rave, celebrate.*
- ✓ Yadah *(H3034): To throw hands upward in praise and thanksgiving.*
- ✓ Tehillah *(H8416): A song of spontaneous praise, often prophetic.*
- ✓ Machowl *(H4234): To dance or whirl in joy.*

In Greek, two key words are:

- ✓ Proskuneo (G4352): To bow in homage, indicating submission.
- ✓ Latreuo (G3000): To serve, minister to, or worship through action and obedience.

Each of these expressions reveals that worship is both posture and practice. It's the raising of hands, the bowing of heads, the movement of feet, the lifting of hearts, and the surrender of will. It is a full-spectrum response to the greatness of God.

For Elina, a young woman from a conservative background in Kerala, these revelations were both exhilarating and terrifying. She had always kept her worship private—internalized, silent, and restrained. But during a prayer retreat, she read through the Psalms and began underlining every mention of dance, shout, or raised hands. She was stunned by how expressive David and others were. One evening, during a time of personal devotion, she felt prompted to stand and dance before the Lord. There was no music, no audience—just her and Jesus. She said afterward, *"I didn't know freedom could feel like that. For the first time, I felt like my worship matched my love for Him."*

Elina now leads worship dance workshops for women who have never known the joy of freedom in movement. She tells them, *"If God made your body, He wants it in worship too."*

Worship That Pleases God: Spirit and Truth

Not all worship pleases God. In Isaiah 29:13, the Lord laments, *"These people come near to me with their mouth and honor me with their lips, but their hearts are far from me."* The tragedy of worship that is only external is that it lacks the intimacy God desires.

True worship begins in the heart and flows outward. It is not performance-driven, but presence-driven. It does not seek to impress, but to express love to the One who is altogether worthy.

This was a painful lesson for Daniel, a talented musician who led worship in a large city church in London. His voice was admired, and his stage presence drew crowds. But over time, Daniel began to feel empty, even during services. One night after leading worship at a major conference, he went home and broke down in tears. "God, why don't I feel You anymore?" he cried.

In the quiet, he felt the Lord speak: *"You've been singing about Me, but not to Me."*

Daniel's journey of repentance and return to intimacy led him to take a break from the platform. He spent months worshipping privately at home—just him and his keyboard, no spotlight, no audience. When he eventually returned to lead again, people noticed something different. There was no show—just glory.

Worship that pleases God cannot be faked. It is spirit-breathed and truth-filled. It is rooted in reverence and intimacy. It may manifest through sound, silence, motion, or stillness—but it always begins in the heart. As Jesus told the Samaritan woman, *"The Father is seeking such worshippers."*

Not worship. Worshippers.

He is seeking people, not performances.

He is seeking you.

Reflection & Activation

- ✓ Spend time meditating on Romans 12:1 and John 4:23–24. Ask God to reveal what areas of your life He is inviting you to surrender as worship.

- ✓ Consider journaling your answer to this question: *"Lord, what does it mean for me to worship You with my whole life—body, mind, heart, and spirit?"*
- ✓ Try expressing your worship in a new way this week—whether through a whispered song, a quiet dance, kneeling in prayer, or even walking silently in nature while praising Him. Let your *life* respond to His worth.

Chapter 2:
The Role of the Body in Worship

In a modern world that often separates the spiritual from the physical, the Church too has at times unconsciously adopted a fragmented view of worship. The heart and soul are deemed sacred; the body, suspicious—too sensual, too emotional, too "fleshly." Yet nothing could be further from the biblical vision of holistic worship. Scripture calls us not just to sing with our lips or believe with our hearts, but to worship God with every fiber of our being—including our bodies.

Worship with All Your Heart, Soul, Mind, and Strength

When Jesus was asked which commandment was the greatest, He didn't hesitate:

"Love the Lord your God with all your heart and with all your soul and with all your mind and with all your strength." – Mark 12:30

This is more than a command; it is a divine design. We were created as unified beings—body, soul, and spirit—meant to glorify God not in parts, but in full. The body is not a barrier to worship; it is a vehicle for worship. Our hands, our feet, our posture, our movement—all of it can express love, adoration, and reverence to the King of kings.

Imagine telling your spouse or child that you love them, but refusing to ever hug them, look them in the eye, or take their hand. Love seeks expression. Worship is love directed toward God—and it too seeks full expression.

This truth transformed the life of Anita, a fifty-eight-year-old widow in Mumbai who had spent most of her life worshipping quietly in the back row of her church. One day, during a time of prayer, she read Psalm 63:4, *"I will lift up my hands in Your name."* She paused. *"I've never done that,"* she thought. That Sunday, she timidly raised one hand during worship. It felt awkward at first, but something shifted inside her. The next week, she raised both. A few months later, she began to dance slowly during her private devotions at home. *"It was as though my worship had found a voice through my body," she later said. "Now, when I move in worship, I feel as though I'm no longer holding back from God."*

Old Testament Examples: When the Body Speaks

From Genesis to Malachi, the Old Testament overflows with physical expressions of worship.

David danced with wild abandon before the Ark of the Covenant in 2 Samuel 6:14:

"And David danced before the Lord with all his might, wearing a linen ephod."

This was not a performance—it was prophetic. It was the king casting aside his royal image and declaring that the presence of God mattered more than public perception. His dance offended his wife, Michal, who saw it as undignified. But David responded, *"I will become even more undignified than this"* (v. 22). His worship was embodied and bold, and it pleased God.

Miriam, the sister of Moses, was the first recorded female worship leader in Scripture.

After the miraculous crossing of the Red Sea, she led the women in worship:

"Then Miriam the prophetess... took a tambourine in her hand, and all the women went out after her with tambourines and dancing." – Exodus 15:20

It was spontaneous. Joyous. Physical. The tambourine in her hand, the rhythm of the dance, the echo of deliverance in every step—this was Israel's first national act of worship, and it was full-bodied celebration.

Ezra and Nehemiah, though known for their leadership and teaching, also brought physical reverence into corporate worship.

In Nehemiah 8:6, when the Law was read, *"all the people answered, 'Amen, Amen!' lifting up their hands. And they bowed their heads and worshiped the Lord with their faces to the ground."* The lifting of hands, the bowing of heads, and the posture of humility were not symbolic gestures—they were active surrender.

These are not isolated events. They are divine patterns, echoing across generations: worship is meant to move us.

New Testament Affirmation of Bodily Worship

The idea that worship is "spiritual" and therefore excludes the body is not only unbiblical—it is dangerous. It reduces the human experience of God to an intellectual or emotional concept, rather than a living, embodied reality.

In the New Testament, Paul writes:

"Do not offer any part of yourself to sin as an instrument of wickedness, but rather offer yourselves to God... and offer every part of yourself to Him as an instrument of righteousness." – Romans 6:13

The phrase "every part of yourself" includes our physical members—hands, eyes, mouth, feet. God does not want to use us merely in theory or emotion; He wants to *inhabit our actions*, *our gestures*, *our movement*.

Later, Paul writes in 1 Corinthians 6:20, *"You were bought with a price. Therefore honor God with your bodies."* The context here is about purity, but the principle applies broadly: your body is sacred real estate. It was purchased by the blood of Jesus, and now serves as a temple through which glory is offered to God.

Mateo, a former breakdancer from Bogotá, Colombia, discovered this powerfully after his radical salvation. For years, he had used his dance talent in nightclubs and street competitions. After encountering Jesus, he gave up the scene entirely—until one night, during worship at a youth retreat, he felt the Holy Spirit whisper, *"What if I gave you that gift for Me?"*

Mateo stepped to the back of the room and began to move—not to impress, but to express. Each step was a prayer. Each movement, an offering. The next week, he shared his story with the church's youth leader and began a dance worship ministry that reached dozens of other young men who never thought their bodies could glorify God.

The False Dichotomy: Spirit vs. Body in Worship

A persistent lie that has crept into the Church is the idea that worship should be only "spiritual," and that bodily expressions are somehow inferior, worldly, or unnecessary. This idea finds its roots not in Scripture, but in ancient Greek philosophy, particularly Gnosticism, which taught that the spiritual realm is good and the physical realm is evil.

But the Bible tells a different story.

God created the body in Genesis 1 and called it good. Jesus came in a body, died in a body, and was resurrected in a body. He ascended in bodily form and will return the same way. The Holy Spirit dwells in our mortal bodies, and our bodies will be raised imperishable on the day of resurrection.

To say that the body is unimportant in worship is to insult the very vessel God created to carry His glory.

And yet, many believers struggle with this tension. Take Angela, a worship leader in rural Uganda. She had a deep desire to dance in worship but had been taught all her life that such expressions were inappropriate for women—especially in public. For years she suppressed the impulse, worshipping silently and rigidly.

But during a women's revival conference, an elder taught about the Hebrew words for worship. When she heard the word "machowl"—to dance—her heart leapt. That night, during the altar call, she stepped forward and began to weep. Then, slowly, almost shyly, she began to move. Not wild or flamboyant—just a gentle sway, a lifted hand, a bowed head. But the freedom was unmistakable.

Later, she said, *"For the first time, I felt like I wasn't just singing about God—I was singing to Him, with all of me."*

True worship does not divide the spiritual from the physical. It unites them. It invites the body to join the spirit in magnifying the Lord. It invites the dancer, the flag bearer, the shofar blower, the one with trembling knees and lifted arms—all to become living instruments of glory.

In doing so, worship becomes not just something we *do*, but something we *are*.

Reflection & Personal Invitation:

- ✓ Take a moment to observe how you use your body in worship. Do you raise your hands? Bow your head? Dance? Kneel? Stand in awe?

  Ask God to show you new ways to offer your body to Him—not just in song, but in posture, in gesture, in motion.
- ✓ Memorize Romans 12:1 and 1 Corinthians 6:20. Let these scriptures shape your theology of worship.
- ✓ Try worshipping God with your body in a private setting—perhaps by kneeling in silence, lifting your hands in your room, or walking in rhythm with praise. Let your body speak what your heart feels.

PART 2:
WORSHIP THROUGH DANCE

Chapter 3:
Dancing Before the Lord

It begins with a rhythm. Sometimes it's in the beat of the drum, the sway of the wind, or the unexplainable stirring in one's soul. Before there were pulpits, microphones, or choirs, there was dance—a primal, powerful expression of worship and wonder. Throughout Scripture, dance is not treated as entertainment or an artistic performance for human applause, but as an act of sacred offering before the Holy One.

To dance before the Lord is to yield one's body as an instrument of praise. It is to say with one's whole being: "You are worthy. You are glorious. And I withhold nothing from You—not even my movement."

Dance as a Biblical Expression

The Bible is not shy about dance.

"Let them praise His name with dancing and make music to Him with timbrel and harp." – Psalm 149:3

"David, wearing a linen ephod, danced before the Lord with all his might." – 2 Samuel 6:14

These are not metaphorical dances. They were real, visible, passionate, and unreserved. The psalmist in Psalm 149 places dance right alongside singing and musical instruments, implying that dancing is as legitimate and spiritual as any song or sound of praise.

David's dance in 2 Samuel was not choreographed or staged. It was spontaneous, prophetic, and deeply personal. The ark of the covenant was finally returning to Jerusalem after years of absence—a visible return of the presence of God. David couldn't help himself. He danced with *all his might*. Not a few careful steps. Not a reserved sway. But a vigorous, vigorous expression of joy that could not be contained.

His wife, Michal, disapproved. She thought he looked foolish, undignified. But David responded:

"It was before the Lord… I will celebrate before the Lord. I will become even more undignified than this…" – 2 Samuel 6:21–22

In essence, David said, *"I wasn't dancing for you. I was dancing for Him."*

Cultural and Spiritual Significance of Dance in the Bible

In the Hebrew culture, dance was never detached from community or covenant. It was often part of the feast days, victories in battle, and times of celebration. It was a sign that something great had happened—and the appropriate response was embodied joy.

We see this in Exodus 15, just after God parted the Red Sea. The Israelites had witnessed a miracle. And Miriam, the prophetess, couldn't just speak about it—she had to *move*.

"Then Miriam the prophetess… took a timbrel in her hand, and all the women followed her, with timbrels and dancing." – Exodus 15:20

Notice—*all the women followed her*. Dance was not a solo act, but a communal testimony of deliverance.

Even in the New Testament, while dance is not mentioned as frequently, the spirit of celebration remains deeply embedded in worship. The story of the prodigal son ends with the father throwing a feast and the sound of music and dancing (Luke 15:25). The symbolism is clear: when the lost return home, celebration breaks out—and dance becomes the natural overflow of restored relationship.

Biblically, dance often serves three primary functions:

- ✓ As celebration of victory
- ✓ As expression of joy and gratitude
- ✓ As a prophetic act of worship and warfare

These are not trivial gestures. They carry spiritual weight and prophetic meaning. Dance says what words cannot.

Breaking the Fear of Man in Movement

But if all this is true, why are so many believers hesitant to dance before the Lord?

One word: fear. *Fear of judgment. Fear of being misunderstood. Fear of doing it wrong. Fear of seeming undignified—just like Michal feared David looked.*

Modern church culture has often been influenced more by human decorum than divine devotion. In many settings, expressive worship, especially dance, is either reserved for children or considered emotionally excessive.

Yet God never demanded dignity in worship—He demanded truth and spirit (John 4:23). The fear of man is a snare that paralyzes the body from responding to the Spirit.

This fear gripped Rebekah Thomas, a 41-year-old banker from London, for most of her Christian life. She was known in her church as refined and quiet—a woman of deep thought and carefully chosen words. Rebekah loved the Lord dearly, but whenever the worship team began to play, she stood still, arms crossed or resting by her sides.

One day, during a conference, a visiting speaker taught on David's dance. Something stirred inside her. She felt as though God was gently tapping her on the shoulder, whispering, *"What's holding you back?"* Rebekah knew. It wasn't theology. It wasn't personality. It was fear—fear of looking foolish.

That night, alone in her room, she played worship music softly and began to move. First, just her arms. Then her feet. Then a gentle twirl. She began weeping. Not out of sadness, but release. Something had broken—the fear of man had lost its grip.

Later, Rebekah shared, "I realized I had silenced part of my worship. I was offering God only what felt comfortable. But that night, I gave Him everything—even my movement. And I've never felt more free."

Her story is echoed across cultures and ages. When people break through the fear barrier, dance becomes not a performance but a proclamation.

A Quiet Woman Who Found Her Voice Through Dance

Naya Elombe grew up in a small township outside Cape Town, South Africa. She was soft-spoken and often overlooked. As a child, she had a limp from a birth defect that made walking difficult and running nearly impossible. Because of this, she never joined in the dances at church during festivals. She would sit in the back and watch, clapping with her hands but never moving her feet.

One night, during a tent revival meeting, a local missionary spoke about the story of Miriam and the Red Sea. He said, *"Your dance is a testimony to your freedom. Don't let your limitations silence your movement."*

The words pierced Naya's heart.

The next morning, Naya stood in her room and said aloud, "Jesus, I may not dance like others, but I will give You what I have."

She began to shuffle slowly in rhythm to a worship song she loved. Her limp was still there, but the joy in her heart overcame her fear. She lifted a scarf in her hand and began to move it as she stepped back and forth. Something powerful happened. She didn't just feel joy—she felt seen. It was as though Heaven was watching, and God was smiling.

Years later, Naya became a worship mentor to girls in her community. She taught them, "Dance isn't about choreography; it's about courage. It's your heart in motion."

To dance before the Lord is to give your body back to its original purpose: glorifying God.

Your arms were made to rise in praise. Your feet were made to leap in joy. Your body is not a prison—it's a temple. And in worship, temples should tremble, move, and rejoice in the glory of their Creator.

Invitation: Try It Yourself

This week, take five minutes in private worship. Play a song that moves your heart. Let go of fear. Begin to move—however gently, however awkwardly. Let your heart lead your body. You may be surprised by the joy that arises.

Remember: God is not grading your moves. He is receiving your offering.

Chapter 4:
Dance in Modern Worship

Dance is not a relic of ancient Israel. It is not merely a cultural artifact preserved in scriptural archives. In the hands of the Spirit-filled believer, dance remains a living, breathing instrument of divine communication—capable of intercession, warfare, prophecy, and intimate communion with God.

As churches across nations rediscover expressive worship, a fresh wave of Spirit-led dancers are rising—moving not for applause, but as vessels for the glory of God. But with this rise also comes confusion: Is it performance or worship? Entertainment or warfare? Is dance merely artistic, or is it also prophetic?

This chapter answers those questions and more, restoring the sacred place of dance in modern worship.

Differences Between Performance and Prophetic Dance

The greatest tension in worship dance today lies in the heart: Whom are we dancing for?

A performance is choreographed for the audience; a prophetic dance is birthed for the Lord. The distinction is not always visible in the movement itself, but in the intent, preparation, and atmosphere it carries.

Performance dance draws attention to the dancer's skill. It is rehearsed, often costume-driven, and aims for artistic impact. It may be moving and even beautiful—but if God is not the central audience, it ceases to be worship.

By contrast, prophetic dance is a yielded act. It may include rehearsed or spontaneous movement, but its origin is always God-breathed. The dancer becomes a vessel—moving as an extension of God's voice in the room.

Biblical Reflection:

In 2 Chronicles 20, when Jehoshaphat faced a vast army, the singers and worshippers were sent ahead of the army. Though the text doesn't mention dance explicitly, ancient Hebrew praise often included movement with music. The principle remains: Worship was used as spiritual warfare, and victory came not through the sword, but through obedient worship.

In a prophetic act, a dancer may strike the ground to declare breakthrough (like Elisha striking arrows in 2 Kings 13), or move in a circle to reflect God's covenant, or sway like wind to represent the movement of the Spirit.

Prophetic dance speaks. And when done in alignment with heaven, it shifts atmospheres.

Dance as Intercession, Warfare, and Prophecy

When a worship dancer begins to move in obedience to the Holy Spirit, something powerful happens: the movement becomes more than expression—it becomes intercession.

1. **Intercession Through Dance:**
   Dancing in intercession is not about emotional gestures; it's about carrying God's burden in movement. The dancer becomes a living prayer—pleading, praising, or groaning through motion.
   "Likewise, the Spirit helps us in our weakness... the Spirit Himself intercedes for

us with groanings too deep for words." – Romans 8:26

A dancer may kneel, stretch upward, circle with arms outstretched, or move slowly in lament. These motions can be God's answer to a congregation too weary to pray.

2. **Dance as Warfare:**

   In Exodus 17, when Moses raised his hands, Israel prevailed. Physical action aligned with divine authority. In modern worship, raised arms, stomping feet, and twirling can function as spiritual declarations of God's dominion.

   One dancer, *Jethro Carvalho* from Goa, India, shared how during a worship night he felt led to leap and stomp during a time of heavy intercession. Unknown to him, a woman in the congregation had been battling suicidal thoughts. The sound of his feet—combined with the cry of the music—was like thunder to her soul. She later testified, "I felt demons leave my mind the moment he danced. God fought for me through his feet."

3. **Dance as Prophecy:**

   Prophetic dance reveals what God is doing now. It's a visual revelation. Movements may come in dreams, or spontaneously as the dancer senses the Lord's promptings.

   In Ezekiel 37, God tells the prophet to prophesy over dry bones. Sometimes dancers are called to do just that—not with words, but with steps and turns and gestures that release life.

Guidelines for Liturgical and Spontaneous Dance
Worship dance must always be rooted in reverence and discernment. Whether liturgical (planned) or spontaneous, it must:

- ✓ Glorify Christ, not the dancer.
- ✓ Flow with the Spirit and the leadership of the service.
- ✓ Be clothed in modesty—physically and spiritually.

Liturgical dance, choreographed to songs, often suits festivals, special services, or corporate declarations. It requires rehearsal, unity, and a clear message.

Spontaneous dance, on the other hand, may arise during deep worship. Here, the dancer must be sensitive—not interrupting the flow, but aligning with it.

Tamira Obong, a worship dancer in Lagos, Nigeria, said, *"I always pray: 'Lord, don't let my feet move unless You're moving.'* There are times I wanted to dance, but the Spirit said, *Wait.* And other times when I was hesitant, He said, *Now.* Dance is worship—not spotlight."

Action Plan: Developing a Worship Dance Ministry

Personal Preparation: Holiness, Skill, Sensitivity
Worship dance ministry starts in the prayer closet, not on the stage. Anyone desiring to lead in movement must cultivate:

- ✓ **Holiness**: A life consecrated to God. Dance is a priestly act.
- ✓ **Skill**: Practice is not fleshly—it's faithful. David was anointed, but also skilled (1 Sam 16:18).

- ✓ **Sensitivity**: Dancers must know the Spirit's voice and timing.

Lina Monroe, a 27-year-old from Melbourne, Australia, began a dance ministry only after fasting for three months and studying Scripture deeply. "I didn't want to just move," she said. "I wanted my movement to be anointed."

Starting a Dance Team: Training, Modesty, Flow with the Holy Spirit

Launching a worship dance ministry requires both structure and spiritual flow:

- ✓ **Vision & Leadership**: Clearly define the purpose—worship, not performance.
- ✓ **Training**: Teach biblical foundations, posture, timing, and techniques.
- ✓ **Dress Code**: Ensure attire honors God and protects from distraction.
- ✓ **Rehearsal & Prayer**: Each session should include intercession.
- ✓ **Submit to Authority**: Flow with your worship leader and pastoral covering.
- ✓ **Unity with Music**: Learn to interpret the rhythm, message, and direction of songs prophetically.

Prophetic Acts Using Dance

Dance can accompany prophetic actions like:

- ✓ **Circling the altar seven times** for breakthrough (Joshua 6)
- ✓ **Waving scarves or flags** in rhythm with heaven's sound
- ✓ **Lifting arms in Y-shape** to declare open heavens

- ✓ **Stamping feet** to war against injustice and declare territory

Carlos Ramirez, a worship leader from Argentina, once choreographed a dance symbolizing dry bones rising. During the altar call, over 80 people came forward. "They saw what God was doing," he said, "before they heard it."

Dance, a Living Language of Worship

God is raising dancers—not just skilled in movement, but sensitive in spirit. The language of movement is not extinct. It is being reborn in sanctuaries, fields, homes, and tents of worship across the globe.

When we dance with purity, precision, and prophetic insight, we move Heaven's heart and shake Hell's gates.

You may not be a trained dancer. You may not even be coordinated. But if you love Jesus and are willing, your movement—however simple—can become a wave of glory.

PART 3:
WORSHIP WITH FLAGS & BANNERS

Chapter 5:
The Power of Banners and Flags

There are times in worship when words fall short—when the soul yearns to proclaim something beyond the grasp of speech. It is here that banners and flags become divine instruments—visual declarations raised not just with hands, but with hearts that burn for the King.

In many modern churches, banners and flags have been dismissed as unnecessary or theatrical. But a closer look at Scripture reveals a different truth: God Himself is a banner, and His people have long raised physical symbols to represent His presence, power, and promises.

This chapter reclaims the sacred ministry of flags and banners—not as decorative accessories, but as spiritual weapons and prophetic proclamations.

Scriptural Foundations

From Genesis to Revelation, banners appear as significant spiritual markers. In the Hebrew Bible, the word "nes" often translated as "banner" or "standard," refers to an ensign lifted up to rally, to proclaim, or to declare identity and allegiance.

In Exodus 17:15, Moses builds an altar and names it Jehovah-Nissi—"The Lord is my Banner"—after God grants Israel victory over Amalek. This is not a metaphor. Moses physically raised the staff of God in battle, and when his arms were lifted, Israel prevailed. The lifting of a standard was a visible declaration: God is fighting for us.

Isaiah 11:12 prophesies that God "will raise a banner for the nations and gather the exiles of Israel." Here, the banner symbolizes God's gathering power—a signpost of salvation.

In Psalm 20:5, David proclaims, *"May we shout for joy over your salvation, and in the name of our God set up our banners!"* The banner here is tied to worship, joy, and prophetic declaration.

Even in the intimacy of Song of Solomon 2:4, the beloved says, *"His banner over me is love."* The flag becomes a covering of identity and affection, not just a call to war.

Clearly, in both times of war and worship, God's people are a banner-raising people.

Symbolism of Colors, Movements, and Shapes

Flags and banners carry a **visual language**. Each color, shape, and movement can reflect divine truths.

- ✓ **Red** may signify the **blood of Jesus**, war, or redemption.
- ✓ **Blue** often represents **heaven, revelation, and intimacy with God**.
- ✓ **Gold** reflects **glory, kingship, or holiness**.
- ✓ **White** speaks of **purity and victory**.
- ✓ **Purple** signifies **royalty and priesthood**.

Movements also carry meaning. A flag waved high over the head can signify exaltation and victory. A sweeping motion may represent cleansing or the moving of the Spirit. Spiraling can symbolize ascension, intercession, or breakthrough.

The shapes matter too. A sharp triangle may represent the Trinity, while a flowing, ribbon-like flag may symbolize the river of God. There's no legalism here—but intentionality is key. Every flag, every motion, is a declaration.

When done in the Spirit, these actions are not performance. They are prophetic gestures—messages in motion.

Raising a Banner: Warfare and Declaration

Just as a military force raises a flag to claim territory, believers raise flags in worship to declare spiritual authority.

In the spiritual realm, raising a banner is like drawing a line in the sand. It says: "This ground belongs to the Lord." It is a prophetic act of alignment with Heaven and defiance against darkness.

In Numbers 2, each tribe of Israel is assigned a standard—a banner that marked their place in the camp. These banners were not for show; they were for order, identity, and remembrance. When Israel moved, the banners led the way.

Even today, banners can lead in worship, in processions, and in intercessory prayer. They speak without words. They signal allegiance, announce prophetic truths, and break the atmosphere open for the move of God.

The Young Girl Who Raised a Flag and Broke Generational Curses

Her name was Adira Jameson. She was 17, soft-spoken, and rarely made eye contact. Growing up in a fractured home in Kingston, Jamaica, Adira had watched her mother battle depression and her older brother slip into gang life. Worship at her local church had always been her refuge—but she never imagined she would be part of it.

One Sunday, the church hosted a weekend of worship workshops. The final session was about flag ministry. Adira didn't want to go, but her mentor,

Sister Glenda, gently nudged her. "Child," she said, "sometimes you don't find freedom with your mouth. Sometimes your hands have to declare it."

During the session, Adira learned about the meaning of colors, the significance of motion, and how flags had been used throughout Scripture. But what stirred her most was when the leader said, "Sometimes the enemy holds a family captive for generations—until one person rises to lift a banner in the name of Jesus."

Something inside her broke.

That night, during the worship service, Adira picked up a crimson flag trimmed with gold. She felt unworthy. Her hands shook. But as the worship swelled, she heard what felt like a whisper deep in her spirit: "Lift it high. I'm with you."

As she raised the flag and began to move, a heat filled her chest. She wept, not because she was sad, but because she felt something break. The flag sliced through the air like a sword. Her movement became bold, almost fierce. In the Spirit, she was cutting ties, declaring freedom, releasing victory.

Others in the room later testified that they felt chains breaking during her movement. Her mother gave her life to Jesus the next week. Her brother walked into the church a month later, desperate to be delivered from a gang debt. God covered him.

Adira wasn't trying to be seen. She was raising a banner—not of fabric, but of faith and fire.

Today, she leads the flag ministry at her church. She teaches young girls like her that worship isn't always loud—but it is always liberating.

A Call to Lift the Standard

Flags and banners are more than art. They are standards—raised in the natural, but shaking the supernatural. To wave a flag in worship is to proclaim, "Here, we declare the Lord's victory. Here, we stand under His name. Here, we shout that love has won."

As Isaiah wrote: *"He will lift up a banner for the nations."* (Isaiah 11:12)

The question is—will you lift it with Him?

Whether in a crowded sanctuary, an open field, or a quiet bedroom—lift your banner. Let the colors speak. Let the movement sing. Let Heaven see, and Hell tremble.

Chapter 6:
The Practice of Worship with Flags

Worship through flags is not merely an artistic expression; it is a holy assignment. When someone waves a flag before the Lord, they are not simply performing—they are proclaiming, interceding, and enforcing spiritual realities in the atmosphere. It is a sacred ministry that requires understanding, intentionality, and spiritual alignment.

This chapter will guide the reader into the practical side of flag worship—how to choose, use, and steward flags for worship, intercession, and warfare, and how to build a ministry that honors the Lord with beauty, excellence, and spiritual integrity.

Choosing Flags: Size, Fabric, Symbolism

The physical design of a flag plays a significant role in its function. Different sizes are used for different environments. A flag meant for a large sanctuary must have strong visibility and structure, while one used for personal soaking worship may be smaller and flowing.

Fabric choice matters. Flowy, lightweight fabrics such as silk or organza offer ease in movement and can create beautiful trails that enhance visual worship. Heavier materials, like brocade or satin, offer bold visibility and weight, useful for powerful, declarative acts such as warfare.

For example, when Judah in the wilderness marched under its tribal banner, each standard was crafted with color and emblem appropriate to the tribe's identity (Numbers 2). This teaches us that our flags should not be random, but reflective of the message being carried.

A worshipper might choose a red silk flag edged with gold to declare redemption and the glory of God. Or a royal purple flag with a lion to represent Christ the King, the Lion of Judah. The visual message is often as powerful as the verbal.

Colors & Their Biblical Meanings

Colors carry deep scriptural significance. When used prayerfully, they become living metaphors of Heaven's truths. Here are a few core meanings drawn from biblical symbolism:

- ✓ **Red**: Represents the blood of Jesus, atonement, deliverance, and warfare. (Exodus 12:13; Revelation 12:11)
- ✓ **Gold**: Symbolizes glory, divine nature, and kingship. (Exodus 25:11; Revelation 21:18)
- ✓ **Blue**: Stands for heaven, revelation, the Word, and spiritual authority. (Numbers 15:38; Ezekiel 1:26)
- ✓ **Purple**: Denotes royalty, priesthood, and kingdom identity. (Judges 8:26; Mark 15:17)
- ✓ **White**: Reflects purity, righteousness, and victory. (Revelation 19:14)
- ✓ **Green**: Symbolizes new life, growth, and healing. (Psalm 52:8)
- ✓ **Black**: Often used to break curses, represent repentance or mourning, but also deep mystery and reverence. (Lamentations 5:10; Jeremiah 8:21)

Flag worshipers should ask the Holy Spirit before each session, *"What color speaks the message You want declared today?"* It's not about fashion—it's about function and faith.

Types of Flag Movements: Warfare, Soaking, Victory, Intercession

Different movements carry different meanings in the spirit realm.

- ✓ **Warfare movements** are strong, aggressive, and authoritative. Think of flags slashing through the air or circling rapidly around a person being prayed for. They declare victory, break oppression, and confront darkness—like Jehoshaphat sending worshippers ahead into battle (2 Chronicles 20:21).
- ✓ **Soaking movements** are gentle, flowing, and healing. These are often slow, wave-like motions. They mirror the movement of the Holy Spirit over the waters in Genesis 1:2 and bring comfort and restoration.
- ✓ **Victory movements** often involve lifting the flag high and wide, moving in circular, upward patterns. It's the spiritual equivalent of the standard being raised after the battle has been won, like the Israelites rejoicing after crossing the Red Sea (Exodus 15).
- ✓ **Intercessory movements** are intentional, strategic, and often low to the ground—touching the earth with the flag as if claiming territory or cleansing the atmosphere. These acts are deeply prophetic, inviting Heaven to break into earthly circumstances.

Each movement is a visual prayer. A flag is not a prop—it is a weapon and a proclamation.

Safety, Order, and Unity in Worship

Because flag worship is physical and often performed in communal spaces, it is essential to cultivate an atmosphere of order, safety, and mutual respect.

Worship leaders and flag teams should ensure that:

- ✓ There is enough space for flag movement, especially during corporate worship.
- ✓ Clear communication exists between the flag team and musicians or platform leaders to avoid distraction or disorder.
- ✓ Flag bearers are taught to move with humility, never to draw attention to themselves but to point hearts to God.
- ✓ Modesty in clothing and choreography is maintained. We worship in spirit and in truth—not in spectacle.

In 1 Corinthians 14:40, Paul reminds us, *"Let all things be done decently and in order."* Even spontaneous movement can flow within boundaries of honor and sensitivity.

Action Plan: Building a Flag Ministry

Materials Needed

A simple yet effective flag ministry can begin with just a few elements:

- ✓ **Flags**: Start with 3–4 sets of flags in key symbolic colors.
- ✓ **Dowels or Rods**: Smooth, lightweight, and sturdy poles to hold the flags.
- ✓ **Storage**: A portable case or closet to store flags neatly and keep them in good condition.
- ✓ **Design Materials**: For creating handmade banners (fabrics, paints, scissors, adhesives).

As the ministry grows, custom designs and prophetic banners can be added based on themes and revelations given by the Holy Spirit.

Biblical Curriculum for Training

A foundational curriculum should include:

- ✓ The Theology of Flags: Scriptural study of banners, colors, and prophetic acts.
- ✓ Worship as Warfare: Understanding spiritual authority and how flags engage the unseen realm.
- ✓ Symbolism and Color Language: Teaching the biblical meaning of colors and patterns.
- ✓ Movement and Practice: Training in posture, movement, safety, and choreography.
- ✓ The Heart of a Worshipper: Discipleship on humility, prayer, and personal holiness.

This training ensures the team carries not only technique—but also truth.

Protocol in Services & Events

Protocols are not restrictions—they are honor systems that help worship flow smoothly:

- ✓ Flag ministry members should arrive early to pray and discern the spiritual atmosphere.
- ✓ They should submit to the worship leader or pastor, always moving in unity and under spiritual covering.
- ✓ Flags should not be raised during solemn, contemplative moments unless Spirit-led.
- ✓ When ministering at other churches or events, ask permission from leadership before using flags. Honor opens doors.

Example: Caleb & the Coat of Many Colors

Caleb Fernandez, a 45-year-old mechanical engineer from Kochi, had never seen himself as a worshipper—much less a flag-bearer. But when his teenage daughter passed away in a car accident, grief hollowed him out.

Six months later, he was invited to a men's retreat. During one of the evening sessions, a leader brought out a set of flags and began to teach on worship through movement. Caleb felt awkward, even foolish. But something drew him to a multicolored flag at the back of the room—one stitched together from many pieces of silk.

"I don't know why," he whispered, "but I feel like this is Joseph's coat... and I'm supposed to pick up the story again."

The leader nodded, sensing the Spirit. Caleb lifted the flag timidly. At first, his movements were slow, uncertain. But as the worship music swelled, he began to move with a freedom he hadn't felt in months. The multicolored flag swirled like Joseph's mantle, and Caleb wept openly—declaring restoration, not only for his heart but for his family's legacy.

Today, Caleb leads a healing and restoration flag ministry at his church. Every session ends with one message: "God gives beauty for ashes—and the flag is His banner of hope."

The Flag That Proclaims

The practice of flag worship is not a modern invention, nor is it an elite ministry for dancers or artists. It is a return to biblical expression—a reclamation of sacred movement and prophetic proclamation.

The flag, when held with reverence and understanding, becomes a voice—a cry lifted not just to Heaven, but from Heaven into the earth.

It says: *“Lift up a standard for the people.”* (Isaiah 62:10)
It invites us to join the Lord’s army—not with swords, but with silk and surrender.

PART 4:
WORSHIP THROUGH STAFFS
(Sticks/Poles)

Chapter 7:
Staffs in Scripture

From the earliest pages of Scripture, the staff appears not just as a physical support for walking, but as a symbol of authority, divine leadership, intercession, and supernatural intervention. More than a tool, it is a spiritual emblem—a visual and tangible representation of God's power in human hands.

The staff in worship is not about theatrics. It's a prophetic act rooted in Scripture, a reminder that God empowers His servants to carry His authority and release His will into the earth.

Moses' Rod – An Instrument of Divine Commission

When God called Moses from the burning bush in Exodus 3 and 4, He didn't ask for a theological dissertation or polished oratory. Instead, He asked, *"What is that in your hand?"* (Exodus 4:2)

It was a staff—ordinary, common, and familiar.

But when God told Moses to cast it on the ground, it became a serpent. Then, as he obeyed and picked it up again, it returned to being a staff. In that moment, the rod ceased to be just Moses' walking stick—it became the "Rod of God" (Exodus 4:20), consecrated and anointed for divine work.

This staff would go on to part the Red Sea, bring water from a rock, and stretch over Egypt as plagues were declared. It wasn't magic. It was obedient partnership with God's voice.

Moses' rod teaches us that in the hands of the called, even the simplest object becomes a conduit for Heaven's agenda. When we lift the staff in worship, it is an act of declaring, *"Lord, I stretch out what is in my hand for Your purpose. Work through me."*

Aaron's Budding Rod – A Sign of Chosen Leadership

Later, in a moment of dispute about priestly authority, God commanded that each tribal leader bring a staff with their name inscribed on it. These rods were left overnight in the Tent of Meeting.

The next morning, only Aaron's rod had budded, blossomed, and borne almonds (Numbers 17:8). In a single night, a dead piece of wood had become a living branch—proving that true spiritual authority is confirmed by fruit and life, not by position or debate.

This rod was kept inside the Ark of the Covenant as a lasting sign of God's chosen leadership.

When we lift staffs in worship today, we are echoing that message: True authority comes from intimacy with God. A worshipper holding a staff must do so with humility, understanding it is not a symbol of personal greatness, but of God's calling, choosing, and presence resting upon them.

The Shepherd's Staff – Jesus and His Pastoral Image

Jesus identified Himself in John 10 as the Good Shepherd, who lays down His life for the sheep. The shepherd's staff or rod was not merely for walking—it was for guiding, protecting, and rescuing.

In Psalm 23:4, David says, *"Thy rod and thy staff, they comfort me."* This dual tool carried symbolic weight: the rod could correct or defend, while the staff with its curved hook could draw a sheep back from danger.

The staff in worship can be wielded to declare guidance, covering, correction, or calling. It becomes a visual intercession—pleading with the Lord to shepherd a wayward generation or guiding people back to green pastures.

When a worshipper lifts a staff in today's context, they aren't just expressing authority—they are stepping into pastoral intercession, inviting the Shepherd King to draw His people close once again.

"The Staff of Intercession That Changed a City"

Rehema D'Souza was a 62-year-old retired nurse living in a bustling coastal city. Her life was simple: early morning prayers, neighborhood visits, and occasional hospital volunteering. She wasn't a public figure. She didn't sing on the worship team. She was, as most would describe her, *"a quiet praying woman."*

But Rehema carried a deep burden for her city. The rise in youth suicides, drug use, and domestic violence had become unbearable. One night during intercession, she had a dream. In it, she saw herself standing on a hill just outside the city, holding a wooden staff, praying and declaring life over the streets below.

When she awoke, she went to her backyard, broke a long guava branch, and cleaned it. She sanded it, anointed it with oil, and carved the word "CHAYIM" into the side—Hebrew for *life*.

Every Friday at dawn, she would climb the small hill near a convent, lift the staff to the east, and begin to pray. No one saw her. No one joined her. But in the spirit, Heaven noticed.

Six months later, strange things began to happen. A notorious gang disbanded after their leader gave his life to Christ. A new rehab center was launched by a Christian businessman. The suicide rate dropped by nearly 40% over the next year.

One day, a young woman named Priya stumbled upon Rehema on the hill and asked, *"What are you doing?"*

Rehema smiled gently and replied, *"Lifting up the Shepherd's staff for my city. I'm reminding the darkness Who is in charge."*

Today, her staff stands in a glass case at her local church, with a plaque that reads:
"A Rod of Intercession. One woman. One city. One Shepherd."

The Rod is Still in God's Hand

In Isaiah 11:1–4, we read of the prophetic image of the coming Messiah, *"A shoot will come up from the stump of Jesse… with righteousness He will judge… and with the rod of His mouth He will strike the earth."* This rod, this scepter, this staff—still lives.

Every time a worshipper lifts a staff, they are partnering with God's justice, leadership, and restoration. It is not an accessory. It is a weapon of intercession, a declaration of divine order, and a call for Heaven to invade earth.

Worship with staffs must not be rushed or mimicked. It must be birthed in intimacy, Scripture, and spiritual weight. For those called to carry it, the staff becomes not just something they hold—but something they become: a branch in the hand of the Lord, bearing fruit that lasts.

Chapter 8: Staffs in Worship Today

In a world increasingly driven by the intangible—digital, conceptual, abstract—worship with staffs brings the physical and prophetic together. The staff, rooted in Scripture, remains a relevant, vibrant, and anointed symbol in modern worship, especially when used with spiritual discernment, scriptural clarity, and heartfelt reverence.

The ancient becomes new when faith-filled hands lift what once guided sheep, parted seas, and confirmed priesthoods. Today, the staff is again rising—not as a relic of the past but as a prophetic tool for visual declaration, spiritual warfare, intercession, and reclaiming identity, particularly among men.

The Staff as Symbol in Warfare and Prophetic Acts

The staff is not just a stage prop. In Scripture, it consistently symbolized God's authority vested in man. When Moses stretched out his rod over the Red Sea, it was not merely a gesture—it was an act of obedience that released supernatural intervention (Exodus 14:16). When he raised his staff during Israel's battle with Amalek, it became a tool of intercession; as long as it was lifted, the Israelites prevailed (Exodus 17:11–12).

Today, a staff in the hands of a worshipper can still symbolize divine covering, God's word, and heavenly order being declared into chaos. In prophetic worship, a staff might be planted into the ground as a declaration of claiming territory for the Kingdom. It can be raised during prayer as a sign of agreement with Heaven's will. It can be moved in prophetic choreography to mirror the movement of angelic hosts or to represent the sweeping authority of God's Spirit.

When used with reverence, the staff becomes a visual sermon, communicating divine truths in the language of motion.

Movement with Staffs: Visual Declarations of Truth

Worship is not always about words. In a generation longing to see the Gospel expressed, visual worship becomes a bridge between heart and Heaven. Movement with a staff is not merely artistic—it's deeply prophetic.

A slow, sweeping motion from east to west might signify God's eyes roaming across the earth (Zechariah 4:10). A downward strike may symbolize binding or breaking in the spirit (Matthew 18:18). The circular spinning of the staff above the head can depict the sovereignty of God, reigning over all.

Just as Aaron's budding rod communicated divine choosing without a spoken word, so too can the movements of a staff declare healing, identity, and authority in ways that bypass language and go straight to the soul.

Reclaiming the Masculine in Creative Worship

There has long been an unspoken void in many churches where male presence in expressive worship is concerned. While many women lead in dance, flags, and prophetic expressions, men often retreat to the background, unsure of their place in this realm.

But biblically, men were often the bearers of the staff. Moses. Aaron. Elijah. Jacob. Even Jesus is metaphorically pictured with a rod and staff (Psalm 23; Revelation 19:15). The staff is an inherently masculine symbol of spiritual responsibility, authority, and guidance.
This chapter is a call to men to rise—not in domination, but in divine representation. Just as the staff was never about human strength but yielded submission, so today, men are invited to take up their staff in worship, not to control, but to lead in humility, warfare, and covering.

"From Carpenter to Carrier: The Man Who Dared to Lead in Worship"

Daniel Nkem, a 39-year-old Nigerian carpenter, had never once danced in church. He led a quiet life with his wife and three children in a rural village near Benin City. Worship, to him, was solemn and internal. He often stood in the back, arms folded, heart silently lifted—but body still.
That changed one Sunday morning when an elderly woman in the congregation began to cry during worship and fell to her knees. The pastor asked anyone who felt led to come and pray over the city's youth—many of whom were being pulled into cults and gang violence.
Daniel felt a strange heat in his palms and then a clear internal nudge: *"Take your measuring rod. It is more than wood in your hands."*
At home that afternoon, he stared at his carpenter's staff—the smooth ash pole he had used for 14 years to measure and level beams. He sanded it. Oiled it. Then carved three words down its side: "Lead, Heal, Guard."

The next Sunday, Daniel walked to the front during worship, lifted his staff, and moved it slowly, intentionally, prophetically. He wept, though no one heard him. *"Lord, shepherd our boys. Discipline the wayward. Call them home."*

That act of obedience sparked curiosity. Over time, more men joined him. Some brought staffs, others spears, some even took up symbolic tools of their trades—plows, levels, rods—turning them into instruments of redemptive representation.

Within a year, a worship movement of male intercessors had formed. Known as "Men of the Measure", they worshipped monthly, lifting staffs over villages, praying as protectors, covering their communities like modern-day spiritual fathers.

How to Use Staffs in Worship

The following steps are for anyone—man or woman—called to express worship through the prophetic use of staffs. It is not about novelty or performance. It is about holy obedience.

DIY or Purchase Options

Many prefer to make their own staff, allowing it to carry personal meaning. Choose a branch or wood that is smooth and strong (like guava, teak, or ash). Sand it, oil it with anointing oil, and inscribe Scripture, names, or phrases that represent your calling (e.g., *"His Rod Comforts Me," "Justice," "Restoration"*).

For those without access to raw wood, staffs can also be ordered from prophetic worship suppliers or crafted using PVC pipes wrapped in linen and oil-treated ropes. Regardless of how it is made, it must be set apart for sacred use.

Spiritual Preparation and Use

Before using a staff in worship:

- ✓ Spend time in prayer and fasting, asking the Lord what the staff is meant to represent.
- ✓ Only bring it into worship after it has been anointed, not just with oil, but with time in God's presence.
- ✓ During worship, remain in sync with the Holy Spirit, not choreography or performance pressure.
- ✓ If you feel led to act prophetically (e.g., strike the ground, wave it over the congregation), seek permission from leadership and always act in order and humility.

Creating a "Rod & Staff" Intercessory Movement

You may be called not just to use the staff yourself, but to raise others who carry spiritual authority through worship.

Here's how to begin:

- ✓ Form a small prayer circle of those who sense a call to visual intercessory worship.
- ✓ Study passages together about staffs, rods, authority, and spiritual warfare.
- ✓ Encourage each person to craft their own staff with intentional prayer.
- ✓ Assign territories—homes, churches, city gates—to intercede over physically and prophetically.
- ✓ Host monthly gatherings to share testimonies, declare scripture, and release prophetic acts with the staffs.
- ✓ Submit everything to your church leadership to ensure covering and guidance.

As the Lord leads, such a movement can revive old wells of spiritual authority, bringing worship and intercession back together in a tangible, Kingdom-advancing way.

The Staff in Worship is a Signpost to God's Power

In a time when the Church must stand boldly against darkness, worship with staffs provides a visible, powerful reminder that God has vested His authority in His people. The staff is not just a stick. It is a symbol of surrender, strength, and the Shepherd who walks with us.

Whether you are young or old, man or woman, timid or bold—if God has placed a "rod" in your hand, lift it in obedience and watch the heavens respond.

PART 5:
WORSHIP THROUGH SOUND – INCLUDING SHOFAR

Chapter 9:
Sound as a Weapon of Worship

There is a mystery in sound—a dimension of divine communication and warfare that transcends language and touches the very core of the spiritual realm. From the opening verses of Scripture, we learn that God did not build the world with His hands—He spoke it into existence. Sound, in the Kingdom, is not noise. It is power, presence, prophecy, and breakthrough.

In this chapter, we uncover the biblical reality of sound as an instrument of worship and war. From the thunderous blast of the shofar to the midnight hymns of apostles in prison, sound shakes foundations, tears down strongholds, and releases God's purposes. It is time for believers to reclaim sound—not just as music, but as a holy weapon wielded in faith.

Walls Respond to Sound: The Fall of Jericho

The story of Jericho is perhaps one of the most astonishing examples of sound as a divine instrument. In Joshua 6, God commanded the Israelites not to raise swords or battering rams but to circle the city in silence for six days. Then, on the seventh day, they were to march around the city seven times, and finally release a blast from the shofar followed by a shout.

The result? The walls of Jericho collapsed.

This was not military strategy—it was prophetic obedience. It was not just a loud sound—it was a sanctified sound. The trumpet (shofar) blast wasn't a signal for war; it was an *act of worship* and an *act of faith*. The shout that followed was not rehearsed—it was a roar of victory before the victory ever manifested.

God did not need Israel's weapons. He needed their worship expressed in obedience. The walls didn't fall because of volume—they fell because of *alignment* with Heaven.

Songs That Break Chains: Paul and Silas in Prison

In Acts 16, Paul and Silas were thrown into the innermost part of a prison, feet fastened in stocks. They were beaten and bloodied. Yet, at midnight, they began to sing hymns. The sound wasn't polished or performed—it was raw worship from wounded hearts.

And Heaven responded.

"Suddenly, there was a great earthquake, so that the foundations of the prison were shaken. And immediately all the doors were opened, and everyone's bonds were unfastened." (Acts 16:26)

Once again, sound—offered not in comfort but in crisis—became the very key that unlocked the impossible. Worship in the dark became warfare in the Spirit. The prison did not just shake for Paul and Silas—every prisoner was set free. Worship creates atmospheres that affect everyone around us.

Sound as a Prophetic Instrument of Breakthrough

Throughout the Bible, God used sound prophetically:

- ✓ Elijah heard "the sound of an abundance of rain" before the rain came (1 Kings 18:41).

- ✓ The Levites sang and played instruments as the ark of the covenant returned to Jerusalem (1 Chronicles 15).
- ✓ At Pentecost, a sound like a rushing wind preceded the arrival of the Holy Spirit (Acts 2:2).

Sound is not merely sensory—it is *sacred*. In prophetic worship, a sound—whether it is a word, a melody, a groan, a blast—can shift spiritual atmospheres, release healing, and birth new realities.

"The Sound That Opened a Womb"

Ruthleen Moyo was a 32-year-old elementary school music teacher in Blantyre, Malawi. She had been married for nine years and had experienced five miscarriages. Her husband, Chisomo, was a kind, faithful man who never blamed her, but Ruthleen often blamed herself. Her womb had become a symbol of unanswered prayer.

Despite her pain, she continued to serve in her small Pentecostal church as the worship leader. Her voice was her offering, and her keyboard her altar. Every Sunday, she led others into God's presence, even when she felt His silence.

One evening, during a women's worship retreat, the Holy Spirit prompted the leader to ask the women to *"sing in the Spirit"*—not in their known tongues, but with spontaneous melody, no words, no lyrics—just sound. As the room erupted in waves of unknown songs and cries, Ruthleen sat in silence. Something felt stuck. Her grief had muted her.

Then a gentle voice whispered inside her: *"Let your pain be your sound."*

She placed her hand over her stomach, closed her eyes, and for the first time in years, sang not with her mouth but with her soul. It wasn't a song—it was a cry. A *wail.* A broken melody filled the room—rising, trembling, groaning with depths too deep for words (Romans 8:26). The other women stopped and listened. Ruthleen kept singing, eyes closed, arms open, womb trembling.

One of the intercessors, not knowing Ruthleen's story, came and blew a shofar near her belly. A sound from heaven collided with a cry from the earth. The atmosphere changed.

That night, Ruthleen slept without weeping for the first time in years.

Three months later, a blood test confirmed what her heart already knew: she was pregnant.

Nine months later, she gave birth to Tadala, which means *"We are thankful"*.

That child, now eight years old, plays violin in church with his mother. Their worship together is no longer shaped by sorrow but marked by a miracle that came through sound.

The Shofar: Heaven's Horn

The shofar, made from a ram's horn, is one of the oldest wind instruments in human history—and one of the most spiritually significant in the Bible.

- ✓ **Used in warfare:** *"When you hear the sound of the trumpet, then all the people shall shout… and the wall of the city will fall down flat."* (Joshua 6:5)
- ✓ **Used to call to worship and repentance:** *"Blow the trumpet in Zion; sound the alarm on my holy hill."* (Joel 2:1)

- ✓ **Used to proclaim victory and Jubilee:** *"You shall sound the trumpet throughout all your land... and proclaim liberty."* (Leviticus 25:9-10)

When a shofar is blown in worship today, it is not just about tradition or drama. It is a spiritual declaration. It breaks confusion. It calls prodigals home. It rebukes darkness. It summons angels. It awakens sleeping hearts.

There is no power in the horn itself, but there is *great power* when God chooses to work through a yielded vessel and anointed sound.

Sound That Shakes, Heals, and Births

Sound is not decoration in worship. It is divine collaboration. When used with discernment, holiness, and faith, sound becomes the spearhead of revival, breakthrough, and deliverance.

God is raising up a generation that understands worship is not confined to melody or lyrics. It is expressed in sound that shifts dimensions—that opens wombs, shakes walls, and unchains prisoners. Heaven is full of sound—thunderings, voices, singing, trumpets—and the earth is invited to join the symphony. Will you become the sound Heaven is waiting to release?

Chapter 10:
The Shofar: Heaven's Alarm

In an age where digital tones and auto-tuned melodies dominate worship experiences, there stands an ancient, rugged horn—primitive in form, yet unmatched in prophetic power. The shofar, carved from the horn of a ram or a kudu, has echoed through the corridors of Scripture as a call to arms, a trumpet of worship, a declaration of freedom, and a warning from Heaven.

It is not merely a musical instrument; it is a spiritual weapon, a divine announcement, a summons to the soul. The shofar is Heaven's alarm clock, waking sleeping hearts, warning wandering souls, and announcing that the King is coming.

What is a Shofar? Biblical Origins & Types

The word *shofar* (שׁוֹפָר) appears more than 70 times in the Hebrew Bible. The first reference is subtle but deeply significant: Genesis 22—when Abraham lifts his eyes and sees a ram caught in the thicket by its horns. This ram becomes the substitute sacrifice, pointing prophetically to Christ. Jewish tradition holds that the horns of that ram became the first shofar.

Shofars were typically made from the horn of a ram, goat, or kudu. The ram's horn is the most biblically preferred, due to its connection with the Abrahamic covenant and God's provision on Mount Moriah.

There are two primary types of shofars still used today:

The ram's horn (*shofar shel ayil*), which is short, curved, and traditional to Israelite worship.

The Yemenite kudu shofar, longer and spiraled, often used in modern worship circles due to its rich, resonant tone.
Both types are sacred when consecrated. Neither is better in the spirit realm—only the purity of the heart behind the breath determines the spiritual weight of its sound.

When and Why Was it Used in the Bible?
The shofar is woven into the fabric of Israel's worship and warfare. In Leviticus 23:24, God institutes a holy convocation on the first day of the seventh month: *"a memorial proclaimed with* blowing of trumpets*, a holy assembly."* This becomes the Feast of Trumpets—Yom Teruah, or the Day of Blasting.
In Joel 2:1, the shofar becomes an alarm: *"Blow the trumpet in Zion; sound the alarm on my holy hill. Let all who live in the land tremble, for the day of the Lord is coming."*
Throughout Scripture, the shofar was used:

- ✓ To **assemble the people** (Numbers 10:3)
- ✓ To **go to war** (Joshua 6)
- ✓ To **declare liberty** (Leviticus 25:9–10)
- ✓ To **crown a king** (1 Kings 1:34)
- ✓ To **signal God's presence** (Exodus 19:16–19)
- ✓ To **announce judgment** (Amos 3:6)

When the shofar sounded, heaven and earth paused to listen.

The Spiritual Meaning of Blowing the Shofar
The act of blowing the shofar is not merely ceremonial—it is prophetic obedience that births divine disruption. It awakens the spirit of man to the presence and purposes of God. Like a divine alarm,

the shofar penetrates slumbering hearts, confronts complacency, and cuts through spiritual fog.

It is also a call to repentance. The prophet Isaiah declared, *"Cry aloud, do not hold back; lift up your voice like a trumpet; declare to my people their transgression"* (Isaiah 58:1). In this, the shofar is not just a sound—it is a confrontation.

It is also used as a weapon of breakthrough, just as in Jericho. The sound of the shofar, when blown under the anointing, disrupts demonic atmospheres, ushers angelic assistance, and creates a moment of kairos—a divine collision with destiny.

The Seven Sounds/Blasts and Their Prophetic Meanings

There are traditionally four primary shofar sounds in Jewish worship, but when prophetically expressed, many worshipers distinguish seven distinct types of blasts, each carrying symbolic power:

1. **Tekiah** – One long, straight blast. Signifies the King's arrival or attention.
2. **Shevarim** – Three broken, sobbing sounds. Symbolizes repentance and brokenness.
3. **Teruah** – A series of nine short staccato blasts. Represents spiritual warfare and **alarm**.
4. **Tekiah Gedolah** – An extended version of Tekiah. It is a final blast of victory, a declaration of triumph and deliverance.
5. **Yobel** – Sound for Jubilee. It heralds freedom and release from bondage.
6. **Zikron** – Sound of remembrance, often used during feasts to recall God's covenant.

7. **Aliyah** – A prophetic ascending tone calling the people to come higher—into deeper worship or revelation.

Each blast is more than symbolic—it is a spiritual activation, when released with discernment.

"The Carpenter Who Blew the Heavens Open"

Noah Matthis, a 47-year-old widowed carpenter from rural Tennessee, had never set foot on a stage. He built porches and repaired old barns. After his wife passed away from cancer, Noah's life became a dull, aching routine. Though a believer, he had grown silent in worship—his grief louder than his faith.

One Sunday evening, a visiting prophetic minister brought shofars and taught on their spiritual purpose. Something stirred deep within Noah. The old man trembled as he approached the altar. He purchased a simple ram's horn not for ministry, but for memory—to remind himself that God still speaks.

Every morning before his work, Noah would kneel beside his workbench, hold the shofar, and whisper, "If You still want to use me, breathe through me." For weeks, he practiced. Alone. Quiet. Until one morning, as he released a blast, his own tears burst forth.

Months later, revival began in his town—not through preaching, but through a construction site. As Noah blew the shofar during prayer breaks on the field, neighbors began gathering. Teenagers knelt. Addicts wept. One blast at a time, the atmosphere shifted.

Noah wasn't a musician. He never taught theology. But his obedience to release sound in faith became the trumpet call for an entirc town to awaken.

Heaven had waited for a surrendered man to blow the alarm.

Action Plan: How to Incorporate the Shofar into Worship

Learning the Blasts

- ✓ Blowing the shofar is a skill, but it is also an *anointed act*. The breath must come from the diaphragm—not unlike deep prayer—and the sound must come not just from lips, but from the spirit.
- ✓ Training should begin in private before public expression. Each blast should be practiced until it is pure and purposeful.

Preparing Your Heart Before Use

No one should blow the shofar in pride or performance. It is not a religious relic or a novelty, but a prophetic act of honor. Before releasing the sound, shofar-bearers should:

- ✓ Repent of hidden sin
- ✓ Dedicate their breath to God
- ✓ Seek His instruction about when and where to release the blast
- ✓ The shofar must never be used to impress. It is to summon Heaven.

When and Where to Use It Biblically

Shofars can be used at the opening of worship gatherings, during times of repentance, for prophetic intercession, or in moments where spiritual breakthrough is needed.

However, it is not to be used carelessly or without sensitivity to the Holy Spirit and spiritual leadership. The shofar is not a tool of hype—it is a vessel of holiness.

Heaven is Sounding the Alarm

In these end times, God is restoring forgotten weapons. Among them, the shofar stands as both a relic of the past and a key for the future. Its voice is not melodic—but it is mighty. Its tone is not sweet—but it is sacred.

May we become a people who don't just play music—but prophesy through sound.

Let the shofar be heard again—not just in pulpits, but in homes, hills, cities, and streets. Not as an echo of tradition—but as a trumpet of transformation.

The alarm is sounding.

Will you blow the trumpet in Zion?

Chapter 11
Sound of Joy – Worship with Tambourines and Percussive Praise

The tambourine is more than a rhythm-maker. It is a *biblical weapon of praise*, a *declaration of joy*, and a *symbol of deliverance*. Throughout Scripture, we see this humble instrument used in moments of divine celebration, prophetic proclamation, and intercessory breakthrough. In many modern churches, tambourines have either been forgotten, dismissed as old-fashioned, or limited to children's ministry. But the biblical weight and prophetic purpose behind the tambourine tell a different story—one worth reclaiming.

A Biblical Instrument of Victory

Our first encounter with the tambourine appears immediately after one of the greatest miracles recorded in the Old Testament: the parting of the Red Sea. In Exodus 15:20, we read: *"Then Miriam the prophetess, Aaron's sister, took a tambourine in her hand, and all the women followed her with tambourines and dancing."*

This moment was not simply a spontaneous celebration. It was *prophetic worship*. Israel had just walked through deliverance. Pharaoh's army had been swallowed by the sea. And the women, led by a prophetess, responded not only in song and dance, but with percussion—with sound that reverberated like a war drum through the wilderness.

The tambourine here became an extension of worshipful expression. It was not quiet, composed, or reserved. It was *loud, rhythmic, and joyful*. It was Israel's way of *declaring in the natural what God had accomplished in the spiritual*.

The Psalms echo this theme repeatedly.

Psalm 149:3: *"Let them praise his name with dancing and make music to him with tambourine and harp."*

Psalm 150:4–5: *"Praise him with tambourine and dancing, praise him with the strings and pipe, praise him with the clash of cymbals..."*

To the psalmists, praise was not sterile. It was dynamic, embodied, and infused with instruments that moved both body and spirit into holy expression.

Even the prophet Samuel in 1 Samuel 10:5 describes worship bands descending from high places with harps, lyres, flutes, and tambourines—accompanied by the Spirit of God falling upon Saul.

In short, the tambourine was *never a filler instrument*. It was integral to warfare, joy, and prophetic atmosphere.

"The Tambourine that Broke the Silence"

Grace Ochieng was a soft-spoken 52-year-old widow who lived in the hills of Nyeri, Kenya. After losing her husband and youngest son in a tragic accident, she withdrew from the church choir, community gatherings, and even prayer meetings. Her once vibrant voice became silent, and her smile faded behind grief.

One Sunday morning, while dusting a forgotten trunk in her storage room, Grace found a dusty, beaded tambourine her son had made for her years ago. Holding it brought tears—tears that turned into whispered prayers. She brought the tambourine to her heart, and for the first time in years, began to tap it softly, singing fragments of old Swahili praise songs through trembling lips.

The next Sunday, Grace walked into church quietly and sat at the back with her tambourine. When the worship team sang, *"You are my hiding place,"* she lifted her hand—and for the first time in years—played her tambourine. Something broke. Not in the room first—but in her spirit.

The pastor later shared that at that exact moment, he had been under a weight of discouragement and felt something shift in the atmosphere. The rhythm, the sincerity, the sound—it was like oil breaking through dry ground.

What began that morning became a ripple in the congregation. Others brought drums. Children returned to dance. An atmosphere of joy returned. Grace hadn't just found her voice—*she had rediscovered her purpose*.

Percussive Praise: Warfare in Rhythm

Rhythmic instruments such as tambourines and hand drums activate something powerful in worship. They are often used to:

- ✓ Celebrate God's victory
- ✓ Break heaviness and depression
- ✓ Shift spiritual atmospheres through prophetic rhythm
- ✓ Unify congregations in joyful praise

Tambourines and other hand-held percussion instruments carry *warfare anointing*. They are disruptive—in the best way. They break monotony, engage the body, and send soundwaves into spiritual realms.

When used under the guidance of the Holy Spirit, they become more than musical additions. They become *prophetic acts*—especially in intercessory gatherings, prayer marches, and street worship.

Action Plan: Reclaiming the Sound of Joy

To incorporate tambourines and percussion into expressive worship, consider this plan as a framework for spiritual, practical, and creative application:

1. Personal Use: Releasing Rhythmic Praise at Home

Start by using a tambourine during your personal devotion or prayer time. Not to perform, but to express. Beat gently while reading psalms aloud or while praying in tongues. Let the rhythm align your heart with heaven's cadence.

Prepare your tambourine spiritually—dedicate it with prayer. Ask the Lord to sanctify it as an instrument of praise and spiritual warfare.

2. Creative Customization

Encourage worshipers to decorate or paint their tambourines with Scripture verses, symbols of God's faithfulness, or tribal patterns representing redemption. This fosters ownership and spiritual meaning.

Materials:

- ✓ Plain tambourine (wooden or plastic)
- ✓ Acrylic paint or permanent markers
- ✓ Oil or anointing spray (optional)
- ✓ Cloth streamers attached to the rim for added movement

3. Corporate Worship Integration

Designate a few trained individuals to lead tambourine worship during high-praise songs. Position them to the side of the altar so as not to distract, but to enhance.

Hold rehearsals where rhythm patterns are taught and spiritual context explained. Align songs with specific rhythms—e.g., slow steady beats for intercession, fast celebratory beats for breakthrough.

4. Workshops for Children and Youth

Invite children and teens to participate in percussive praise. They naturally connect with rhythm. Teach them Psalm 150 and let them experiment with different percussive sounds. Empower them to lead a praise song using tambourines in a Sunday service.

5. Prophetic Application

In prayer meetings or prophetic acts (like Jericho marches or intercessory walks), assign tambourine bearers to walk in rhythm while intercessors pray. The beating of the tambourine becomes a prophetic declaration: *God has given us the land*.

Final Thought

The tambourine, though often overlooked, carries heaven's heartbeat. It was there when Israel was set free. It echoed in temple praise. It danced in David's courts. And it can still rattle chains today.

In *WAVES OF GLORY*, we have explored the physical movements of worship—through dance, sound, banners, staff, and shofar. Let us now ensure we do not forget the *percussive joy* of the tambourine—the laughter of heaven drumming through our hands.

Let every strike declare, *"God is victorious!"* Let every beat carry the echo of Exodus freedom. And let every rhythm open dry hearts to the rain of His glory.

The sound of joy is not a sound of perfection. It's a sound of release. Pick up your tambourine. The dance has only just begun.

PART 6:

BEING FORMED INTO A WORSHIPPER

Chapter 12: Becoming a Worshipper through Expression

Before David ever picked up a sling or a sword, he picked up a harp. Before Miriam danced, she watched the sea split. Before Paul wrote letters, he worshipped in chains. Worship, in the kingdom of God, is not a department of the Church—it is the essence of the believer's identity.

Expressive worship—whether through dance, sound, banners, or posture—is not something reserved for the stage or the sanctuary. It is the overflow of a life lived in awe of God, an offering that comes not from talent, but from transformation. And the journey into expressive worship is not just about what you do—it's about who you become.

Identity First: Worshippers Before Warriors

Before we learn to move, wave, dance, or blow the trumpet, we must learn to *be*. We are not primarily dancers, singers, or intercessors. We are worshippers.

In John 4:23, Jesus said, *"The hour is coming, and is now here, when the true worshipers will worship the Father in spirit and truth, for the Father is seeking such people to worship Him."* He was not looking for skill sets; He was looking for surrendered hearts.

David's worship was not born on the battlefield—it was born in the pasture. In 1 Samuel 16, David was anointed not because of what he had done, but because of who he was when no one was watching.

His private worship made him Heaven's choice long before he was Israel's champion.
True worshippers are not made on platforms. They are formed in obscurity.

Emotional Healing Through Expressive Worship
Many who come to expressive worship do not come from places of strength. They come with stories, scars, and silence. And that is precisely the point. God doesn't require perfection to receive expression. He just requires the truth.
Psalm 30:11 says, *"You turned my mourning into dancing; You removed my sackcloth and clothed me with joy."* This is not a poetic metaphor. It is an emotional transformation through expressive release.
Take, for instance, the story of Camila Rivera, a quiet middle-aged teacher from Bogotá, Colombia. After enduring years of emotional abuse from a controlling spouse, Camila found herself numb. Her faith was intact, but her voice was gone. She would attend church, lift her hands half-heartedly, and return home with a sense of defeat.
One Sunday, during a women's retreat, a speaker invited the women to take flags and move freely before God. Camila stood at the edge of the room, frozen. She had never danced, never moved in worship. It felt ridiculous—until she saw a teenage girl waving a flag with tears in her eyes.
Something inside Camila broke. With trembling hands, she picked up a small purple banner and stepped into the room. At first, her movements were stiff. But with each swing of the flag, decades of silence began to shatter. Her tears flowed, her shoulders shook, and for the first time in years, she felt like a daughter—not a victim.

Expressive worship can become the canvas where God paints healing into broken places. It moves trauma from storage in the soul into surrender before His presence.

Faith Over Fear: Expressing Even When It Feels Awkward

It is not uncommon to feel awkward in expressive worship. Whether it's dancing, waving banners, kneeling, or even weeping—expression always comes with a risk: the fear of man.

But the Bible is clear: *"The fear of man lays a snare, but whoever trusts in the Lord is safe"* (Proverbs 29:25). Fear of judgment is a prison. But worship is freedom.

Ezekiel Omondi, a 26-year-old software engineer in Nairobi, Kenya, never imagined himself as an expressive worshipper. Analytical by nature and raised in a conservative congregation, Ezekiel was taught that true worship was internal and quiet. He believed raising hands or moving was "too emotional."

But one day, while attending a citywide prayer gathering, he watched a young man dance passionately during worship. What caught Ezekiel off-guard was not the dance—it was the **joy** on the man's face.

Something in Ezekiel yearned for that freedom. When the shofar sounded and the worship intensified, Ezekiel—against every voice of self-consciousness—began to move. A small step. A lifted hand. A whispered "yes."

It felt awkward. But it felt real.

He later shared that while he didn't become a dancer overnight, that moment shifted his understanding of worship. It wasn't about public approval. It was about private surrender made public.

Faith is choosing obedience over embarrassment. It is lifting your voice when your flesh wants silence. It is moving your feet when fear says sit still. True worshippers are not fearless—they are faith-full.

Personal Devotion & Expression at Home

Public worship is powerful. But the furnace where expressive worship is forged is in personal devotion. If you cannot move before God alone in your room, you will struggle to move before God in a crowd.

Jesus said in Matthew 6:6, *"When you pray, go into your room, shut the door, and pray to your Father who is in secret."* The same can be said of expressive worship.

Miriam Chao, a 33-year-old nurse in Malaysia, discovered this truth after a long night shift. Exhausted but desperate for God's presence, she played instrumental worship music softly in her apartment. As she knelt by her bed, she felt prompted to rise—not just to pray, but to move.

With no one watching, no stage, no expectations, Miriam began to sway. Her arms lifted, her body flowed, and her worship became a conversation of movement. Her flat became a sanctuary. Her movements, a language only Heaven understood.

That night, she journaled: *"For the first time, I felt like I wasn't just worshipping—I was* being *worship. My body, soul, and spirit aligned as one song before Him."*

This is the call: to become a living sacrifice—not in theory, but in expression. As Romans 12:1 reminds us, *"Offer your bodies as a living sacrifice, holy and acceptable to God, which is your spiritual worship."*

Becoming Before Doing

Before we become expressive worshippers on the outside, we must first allow God to form the worshipper within. It's not about being seen; it's about being true. Worship is not choreography—it is covenant. Not mere movement—but manifested intimacy.

The banners, flags, staffs, and shofars are not the goal—they are the instruments of a heart that burns for God.

And the invitation stands: Will you allow your whole being—body, soul, and spirit—to become His sanctuary?

Chapter 13: Forming a Prophetic Worship Team

Forming a prophetic worship team is not simply about assembling talented individuals with expressive abilities. It is about gathering a consecrated company of worshippers who move, wave, lift, declare, and intercede in alignment with the heart of God and the rhythm of Heaven.

Prophetic worship teams are instruments—not performers. They do not draw attention to themselves, but instead, they help usher the congregation into deeper awareness of God's presence. Their movement, their sound, and their presence are not ornamental—they are prophetic acts, shifting atmospheres, declaring truth, and making space for God to manifest His glory among His people.

The Roles Within a Prophetic Worship Team

Each role within a prophetic worship team carries spiritual weight and must be discerned—not assigned randomly. Just as the Levitical tribe was divided into specific functions in the tabernacle (1 Chronicles 25:1–8), so too should we recognize the unique purpose each person brings to the altar of expressive worship.

In the early church, unity and order were key, even in the outpouring of spiritual gifts (1 Corinthians 14). Likewise, within the prophetic worship team, order is not control—it is a conduit for the Spirit to flow unhindered.

Take the church of New Dawn Fellowship, a small congregation in Cape Town, South Africa. As revival began to stir, the pastor sensed God prompting them to raise a prophetic worship team. It wasn't about stage production—it was about obedience. One by one, God began to highlight people in the congregation: a quiet woman who danced in private, a teenage boy with a burden to blow the shofar, an elderly intercessor with vision during worship, and a young couple who felt called to wave banners.

They were different in age, background, and ability—but united in hunger. That's when the transformation began.

Dancers

Dancers in a prophetic team do not just move to rhythm; they move in response to God's heart. Their posture prophesies. When David danced before the Ark of the Covenant in 2 Samuel 6, he was making a declaration of honor and unrestrained joy. His movement stirred mockery from the flesh (Michal) but was pleasing to the Lord.

Flag Bearers

Flag bearers are not random wavers of color—they are wielders of spiritual symbolism. In Exodus 17:15, Moses built an altar and called it "The Lord is my Banner." When banners are raised today, they become visual declarations of truth, war, peace, identity, and breakthrough.

Shofar Blowers

The blowing of the shofar is not performance—it is proclamation. It announces Heaven's timing, summons God's people to attention, and signals a shift in the spiritual realm (Joel 2:1). Shofar blowers must be sensitive, trained, and yielded—not simply skilled.

Intercessors

Intercessors are the spiritual backbone of the team. They don't always move publicly but cover the atmosphere in private. Like Aaron and Hur who lifted Moses' hands (Exodus 17:12), they lift the arms of the worship team with hidden strength.

When these roles come together—not as isolated acts but as one unified body—they mirror the harmony of Heaven.

Training Spiritually and Practically

Training a prophetic worship team requires both spiritual depth and practical skill. Just as musicians train for excellence, expressive worshippers must learn to steward their role with intentionality.

Spiritual Training involves:

- ✓ Intimacy with God through personal devotion
- ✓ Biblical understanding of worship and prophetic acts
- ✓ Character development: humility, purity, obedience
- ✓ Accountability and openness to correction

Practical Training involves:

- ✓ Movement drills and pattern learning for dancers
- ✓ Understanding color, motion, and fabric dynamics for flag bearers
- ✓ Shofar breath control and tone familiarity for blowers
- ✓ Timed intercession, journaling, and listening prayer for intercessors

Consider Thomas & Leah Ajayi, a husband and wife in Lagos, Nigeria. Thomas had experience as a percussionist, while Leah loved expressive art. When they joined a prophetic team, their leader, Sis.

Naomi, didn't hand them a flag or ask them to dance. She first handed them a journal and a Bible. "You cannot declare what you do not first hear," she said. For three months, their training was private devotion, Scripture memorization, fasting, and team prayer. Only then were they introduced to movement and expression. Today, they mentor other couples, grounding them first in the altar of the secret place before the stage of public worship.

Building Unity, Submitting to Leadership, Flowing with Worship Team

A prophetic worship team must be submitted, not scattered. It cannot function like individual fireworks; it must be a constellation—distinct yet aligned.

Paul exhorted the Corinthians in 1 Corinthians 12 that the body has many parts, and each must work in unity. Prophetic worship teams function best when they submit to leadership, honor one another, and stay yielded to the worship flow of the house.

This means dancers don't move for applause, shofar blowers don't interrupt flow, and flag bearers don't become distractions. The Spirit of the Lord brings order, not confusion.

Pastor Evelyn Sato of a congregation in Osaka, Japan, once shared a story of her team falling into disarray. Each dancer had grown proud of their movement, each flag bearer insisted on their color interpretation. The Spirit stopped moving. Convicted, Evelyn called for a week of prayer and fasting. The team repented, realigned, and rededicated themselves not to expression—but to obedience. The next service, without choreography, they moved in complete unity—and Heaven responded.

Unity is not uniformity—it is shared surrender.

Guidelines for Services and Public Expression

Prophetic worship is powerful—but must be guided by reverence and maturity. Paul's correction to the Corinthian church (1 Corinthians 14:40) remains applicable: *"Let all things be done decently and in order."*

In public settings, prophetic teams should follow certain principles:

- ✓ Always honor the pastoral leadership. If the pastor says pause, you pause.
- ✓ Flow with the worship team's rhythm and sound. Don't move out of sync.
- ✓ Be modest in attire, clear in purpose, and flexible in spirit.
- ✓ Never perform; always minister. The goal is *presence*, not *praise*.

In River of Hope Church, in Calgary, Canada, the team meets 30 minutes before every service to pray—not for performance, but for posture. They ask: "Lord, what are You doing today?" Sometimes they move; sometimes they remain still. But they are always aligned with Heaven.

A Company Formed for Glory

Forming a prophetic worship team is not about showcasing gifts. It is about building an altar—a living one—on which God can rest.

Each dancer, flag bearer, shofar blower, and intercessor is like a stone in that altar. And when placed in unity, in humility, and in reverence, the fire falls.

Prophetic worship is a calling—not a craft. It demands discipline, love, submission, and above all—intimacy with the One we worship.

As Heaven seeks worshippers in spirit and in truth, may we be found among the ones who not only lift our voices but offer our very selves as vessels of glory.

Chapter 14: Warfare & Intercession through Movement and Sound

There are moments in the spiritual realm when words alone are not enough. The weight of warfare, the depth of intercession, and the breakthrough needed in the heavens call for something more—something embodied. In such moments, the Lord releases a divine strategy: not just prayer, but movement and sound in prophetic unity. These acts do not replace prayer; they amplify it, joining earth with heaven in a visible declaration of God's authority.

Jericho Marches & Prophetic Enactments: The Power of Obedient Movement

In Joshua 6, God gave Joshua a strange military instruction: *"March around the city once with all the armed men. Do this for six days... On the seventh day, march around the city seven times... When you hear them sound a long blast on the trumpets, have the whole army give a loud shout"* (Joshua 6:3–5, NIV).

This was not a traditional war tactic—it was a prophetic act of obedience. The Israelites did not shout first; they marched first. They aligned their movement with God's strategy. And when their obedience reached its climax—movement with sound, synchronized and consecrated—the impossible happened. Jericho fell, not by strength, but by surrender to the prophetic.

Similarly, in 2 Kings 13, Elisha instructs King Joash to shoot arrows and strike the ground. His level of obedience in striking the ground would determine his victory over Aram. When Joash only struck three times, Elisha rebuked him: *"You should have struck five or six times... then you would have defeated Aram completely"* (2 Kings 13:18–19). Again, the physical act of obedience held spiritual consequence.

Prophetic movement is not entertainment; it is intercession. It is partnering with Heaven's warfare strategy through embodied declarations.

Strategic Unity: Combining Dance, Flag, Staff, and Sound

When expressive worship is strategically combined, it becomes a multi-dimensional tool of prophetic intercession. Each element—dance, flags, staffs, and sound—carries unique symbolism and impact. When woven together in prayerful unity, they pierce darkness and prepare the way of the Lord.

Imagine the imagery of Exodus 17, when Moses held up his staff during the battle against Amalek. As long as the staff was raised, Israel prevailed. Now consider combining that with Psalm 149:3–9, which links dancing, praise, and the "high praises of God" with the ability to "bind kings with chains and their nobles with fetters of iron." These are not metaphors of mere celebration—they are declarations of spiritual warfare through expression.

A flag raised in intercession can symbolize a divine claim over a territory. A staff struck into the ground can declare authority and establishment. A dance can break oppression, and a sound—whether from voice or shofar—can release prophetic shift.

It is not about the props. It is about the obedient hearts behind them.

A Small Church that Brought Revival through Prophetic Worship

In the sleepy hill town of Sheltorah—a forgotten mining village tucked in the northeast region of India—stood a church of no more than thirty-five members. The congregation of Zion Light Chapel was faithful but weary. Their youth had migrated to cities. Their pastor, Rev. Matthew Thangjam, often battled discouragement, having served there for 18 years without seeing growth.

One evening, during his private prayer time, Pastor Matthew read again the story of Jericho. He paused, sensing the Spirit nudge him: *"What if your breakthrough lies not in more sermons, but in more surrender?"*

That night, he invited a handful of prayer warriors to his home. Among them was Ananya, a widowed teacher with a heart for worship, and Chiko, a quiet 20-year-old who had taught himself the shofar by watching videos on a borrowed phone. There was also Thangboi, a farmer with strong hands and a carved bamboo staff he used for shepherding goats.

As they prayed, Ananya felt led to bring her homemade silk scarf—red, gold, and white—and wave it gently while interceding. Chiko brought his shofar. Thangboi placed his bamboo staff across the room and knelt beside it.

They began meeting weekly—not to rehearse, but to worship. Dance movements emerged organically. Ananya twirled, not for beauty, but to declare the blood and glory of Jesus over the valley. Chiko's blast on the shofar grew bold, releasing an echo through the hills. Thangboi began striking the ground with his staff in intercession—each strike a cry for God to shake their land.

Word spread quietly. Within three months, youth began returning. People reported healing, deliverance, and even demonic strongholds breaking during worship. The villagers didn't understand every movement—but they couldn't deny the power. Pastors from surrounding areas came, not to criticize but to learn.

What changed?

Not the building. Not the program. But the posture.

This was no performance. It was prophetic warfare in motion.

The revival at Zion Light Chapel wasn't marked by fireworks but by deep deliverance and holy awe—a move birthed in a small room by unlikely vessels who offered their bodies, instruments, cloths, and staffs as living sacrifices (Romans 12:1).

A New Era of Intercession

The Church is being reawakened to the integrated nature of worship and warfare. The days of confining spiritual warfare to silent prayers are over. Heaven is summoning a generation who will shout like Joshua, dance like David, wave like Moses, strike like Elisha, and blow like Gideon's trumpet bearers (Judges 7).

In the Book of Revelation, heaven is filled with worship that includes movement, sound, and posture: elders casting crowns, creatures crying "Holy!", and multitudes falling before the throne. If Heaven is expressive, should not Earth be?

Prophetic worship teams are not called to entertain or impress. They are called to war and intercede, using every fiber of their being to invite Heaven's rule.

In cities where darkness prevails, churches must become altars again—where banners are lifted, shofars blown, staffs raised, and feet move in step with God's heartbeat. This is not chaos. This is the orchestrated warfare of Heaven.

As Ezekiel prophesied to the dry bones (Ezekiel 37), and as those bones rattled into alignment through the Word and wind—so today, as prophetic worship teams align, we will see valleys of death become armies of the Lord.

Let every movement count. Let every sound resound. Let every team be forged in unity, purity, and bold obedience. For in this day, God is not just seeking worshippers—He is raising warring worshippers who understand the prophetic power of motion and sound.

The glory will come—not just through preaching—but through the prophetic acts of surrendered worshippers who move when He says move, shout when He says shout, and strike the ground until Heaven breaks through.

PART 7:

GLORY WAVES: LIVING A LIFE OF EXPRESSED WORSHIP

Chapter 15: Hosting God's Presence through Movement and Sound

There is a difference between *visiting* the presence of God and *hosting* it. A visit is momentary; a hosted presence remains. As believers, we are not merely called to encounter God during worship—we are called to become habitations of His glory. When worship is expressed not just with words but through movement and sound, it creates space—sacred space—for God's glory to dwell.

Movement and sound, when surrendered to the Holy Spirit, are not mere expressions—they are *invitations.* They carve out atmosphere, not only in sanctuaries but in living rooms, marketplaces, and even streets. They become prophetic acts, turning ordinary ground into holy ground.

Testimony-Centered Worship: Honoring the Works of God

Psalm 22:3 tells us that God is *"enthroned on the praises of Israel."* But those praises were never shallow chants. They were rich with remembrance. The songs of Israel echoed testimonies of deliverance, conquest, and mercy. Every sound declared, *"This is what our God has done!"*

Expressed worship must be rooted in testimony.

In Revelation 12:11, we are told that the saints overcame *"by the blood of the Lamb and the word of their testimony."* When dance, flags, shofar, or staff movements are inspired by personal or corporate testimonies, they become powerful declarations that shift spiritual climates.

Consider Deborah, the prophetess and judge. In Judges 5, after the Lord gave Israel victory over Sisera, Deborah and Barak *sang* a prophetic testimony. This wasn't performance—it was intercessory declaration. Their song recounted God's might and Israel's obedience. That song likely inspired generational courage.

Testimony-centered worship happens when people don't just move to music—they move in response to God's acts. It might look like a woman waving a gold flag in response to a healing. Or a man dancing with abandon because he was once bound by shame. These are not performances. These are living altars of gratitude.

Creating Glory Atmospheres in Homes, Churches, and Cities

The glory of God is weighty. It doesn't come lightly, and it doesn't linger where it's not honored. The Ark of the Covenant remained in Obed-Edom's house, and Scripture tells us that his whole household prospered during that time (2 Samuel 6:11). Why? Because Obed-Edom hosted the presence with reverence.

Worship through movement and sound creates glory atmospheres—spaces where Heaven touches Earth tangibly. But these atmospheres must be cultivated.

Let's look at the small Indian town of Shalompur—a place nestled along the southern coast. In this quiet community, a middle-aged couple, Jeremiah and Kavitha Daniel, began a Friday evening worship gathering in their home. What began as a few voices and an old guitar grew into something none of them expected.

Kavitha, once hesitant to express herself, began to move with a small silk scarf during spontaneous songs. Jeremiah, a former military officer, began blowing the shofar at the start of their worship. Their teenage daughter Alisha, once depressed and introverted, began twirling in dance during prayer. Soon, flags appeared. Then staffs. Then neighbors. Then miracles.

People reported that when they stepped into the Daniels' house, they felt peace. Children who struggled to sleep began resting deeply. Those battling torment or illness said they experienced a lightness in their hearts. It wasn't about the props—it was about the presence. The movement and sound were gateways, not the goal.

The Daniels didn't build a ministry. They built an altar. An altar that eventually spread. Other homes replicated it. Soon, a dozen houses across Shalompur became hubs of worship, healing, and encounter.

Worship that hosts God's glory will always spill beyond the walls. When a church, home, or city chooses to embrace expressive worship not as a style but as a surrendered act of reverence, the glory comes—and the glory transforms.

From Expression to Encounter

In John 4:23–24, Jesus says the Father is seeking true worshippers, not worship performances. The goal of expressive worship is not the movement or the sound—it is the encounter. A life-changing moment where God shows up, marks you, and never leaves you the same.

Take the story of Derek, a corporate executive from London. For years, he had been skeptical of expressive worship. Flags seemed odd. Dance felt unnecessary. Shofars annoyed him. Until one night, his teenage son invited him to a worship night held in a local warehouse.

Derek came out of love, not faith. But as the worship began, something shifted. A young woman began to dance—clothed in white, moving in gentle circles, tears streaming down her face. A man began waving a deep blue banner overhead. Then, a shofar blast rang out—loud, deep, and piercing.

Derek didn't understand it—but suddenly, he began to weep uncontrollably. Decades of hardened anger broke open. The sounds had pierced the fortress of his soul. That night, he met Jesus in a way he never had before. Not through a sermon. Not through theology. But through the encounter birthed by surrendered expression.

That night, Derek's life changed. He later testified, *"The flags moved the air, but the Spirit moved my heart. I encountered the God I had only heard about."*

This is the essence of expressive worship: it is not just vertical—between us and God—it is horizontal, reaching others. It's not about drawing attention. It's about drawing Heaven.

The Weight of Glory

To host God's presence is to say: *"Lord, You are welcome here—not only in our minds, but in our space."* Movement and sound make room for that invitation to become visible. When believers surrender their bodies, instruments, and tools to the

Lord, something holy happens. The atmosphere changes. Bondages break. Heaven responds.
As Paul writes in 2 Corinthians 4:7, *"We have this treasure in jars of clay to show that this all-surpassing power is from God and not from us."* Expressive worship is the breaking of those jars—the offering up of our weak vessels so that His glory may pour out.
In this next wave of revival, God is not simply raising up speakers. He is raising up hosts—men, women, and children who will welcome His glory through movements of reverence and sound. And as they do, Heaven will move.

Let the dancers rise. Let the flag bearers wave. Let the shofars sound. Let staffs strike. Not for spectacle—but for sanctuary.
We were made to host His glory.

Chapter 16: Preparing for a New Wave of Glory

Worship has always been God's chosen meeting place with humanity. From Eden's walks in the cool of the day to John's vision of thundering praise around the throne, worship has marked both history and eternity. But there are seasons in which God intensifies His presence, calling His people into new waves of glory. These waves are not created—they are hosted, by hearts that have been prepared.

We are in such a time. A time where expressive, prophetic worship is no longer optional—it is *essential*. The Spirit is summoning worshippers not merely to sing or dance but to stand in the gap, to declare, to war, and to carry His glory into every domain of life.

The Prophetic Call to Today's Worshipper

In Exodus 19, God called Israel to gather at the base of Mount Sinai. It was not just for instruction—it was for encounter. God said to Moses, "*Consecrate the people and have them wash their clothes. Be ready by the third day*" (Exodus 19:10–11). Before glory comes, there is always a call to consecration.

This call is upon today's worshipper.

Not all are called to the platform, but all are called to posture. Worship in this hour is a prophetic assignment. It is not for entertainment, nor simply expression. It is for intervention. The worshippers who heed this call will be those who—like the sons of Issachar—understand the times and know what to do (1 Chronicles 12:32). They are not bound by traditions of men, but are led by the Spirit of God.

Let's look at the story of Jonas Ezekiel, a 62-year-old farmer from a remote village in Uganda. Jonas had never received formal education, never led worship, never touched a microphone. But in his morning devotions, as he walked through his fields, he began to sing to the Lord—not the songs he'd heard from missionaries, but his own melodies.

One day, the Holy Spirit instructed him to fashion a staff from the branch of an old fig tree. Jonas obeyed. He began walking the perimeters of his village, lifting that staff and declaring Scriptures aloud. Over time, the atmosphere began to shift. Family feuds dissolved. Crops began flourishing even during drought. A demonic stronghold of alcoholism that plagued the men of the village began to break.

Jonas was not a preacher. He was not trained. But he was called. He answered not with words, but with worshipful obedience—and heaven responded.

This is the prophetic call of this hour: for ordinary believers to host extraordinary glory through obedient, expressive worship.

End-Time Worship and the Role of Prophetic Acts

Jesus, when asked about the end times, spoke of wars, earthquakes, persecution—and then He added something profound in Matthew 24:14: *"And this gospel of the kingdom will be preached in the whole world as a testimony to all nations, and then the end will come."*

But what kind of gospel will the world see? Not merely words. They must see the gospel in motion. The end-time Church must be demonstrative—not for show, but for warfare.

Prophetic acts in worship are not symbolic gestures—they are spiritual legislation.

Take the case of Leora Fernandes, a worship dancer in São Paulo, Brazil. Leora was once bound by fear—her childhood filled with rejection and emotional abuse. She rarely spoke in public, let alone moved. But during a quiet worship night, she felt the Lord ask her to wave a purple flag and kneel before the altar.

As she did, she saw—internally—a vision of shackles breaking. Unbeknownst to her, in that moment, a woman in the congregation who had been battling suicidal thoughts felt something lift. Deliverance came not through sermon, but through prophetic movement.

Prophetic acts are not mere accessories in end-time worship—they are weapons. As the battles of this age grow more spiritual, more invisible, the responses must become more spiritual and visible. Movement. Sound. Staffs. Banners. Dance. All choreographed by heaven.

The Lord is raising worship warriors—those who know how to stand between the porch and the altar (Joel 2:17), those who know how to lift a sound that silences the accuser, and those who know how to act prophetically even when it seems foolish in the eyes of men.

Vision for Generations to Come

The wave we prepare for is not just for us—it is for our children and our children's children.

Psalm 145:4 declares, *"One generation shall commend your works to another, and shall declare your mighty acts."* Glory must not stop at an event—it must become a legacy.

Let us consider the fictional story of Anaya George, a 39-year-old single mother in Atlanta. Anaya had a daughter, Zara, age 10, who had trouble focusing in school and was diagnosed with social anxiety. Traditional worship settings overwhelmed her.

One afternoon, Anaya, inspired by a conference on expressive worship, brought home a small blue flag and a CD of instrumental worship. She invited Zara to simply wave the flag to the music, just as play. To her surprise, Zara responded with joy. Every evening, Zara would wave that flag, her small feet twirling, her face beaming.

Months later, a school teacher called Anaya and said, *"I don't know what's changed, but Zara is like a new person—confident, calm, and more focused."* What changed? Atmosphere. Zara had been trained in glory. Not by lectures, but by expression.

Children raised in atmospheres of expressive worship will carry the presence of God into schools, boardrooms, and nations. They will not be afraid of spiritual darkness because they will have learned how to shift the atmosphere with a sound, a gesture, or a prophetic act.

We must teach them that worship is not only what happens at the altar—it's what happens when their feet dance in faith, their hands wave banners in joy, and their voices release heaven's decree.

The Wave Is Coming

Throughout history, every wave of God's glory has looked different. The Tabernacle of David brought continuous praise. The Upper Room brought tongues of fire. The Azusa Street Revival released the power of the Holy Spirit with groans and wails. And this next

wave? It will be marked by movement and sound—expressions that align earth with heaven.
But only the prepared will carry it.

- ✓ Will you respond like Isaiah: “Here am I, Lord—send me”?
- ✓ Will you lead your family, your home, your church into spaces where the presence is not just felt—but hosted?
- ✓ Will you raise your flag, blow your shofar, lift your staff, and dance your prophetic dance not for applause—but for encounter?

A wave is rising. The Spirit is stirring. The sound is awakening.
Prepare the way. Prepare your heart. Prepare a generation.
Let the worshippers arise, for the King of Glory is coming through the gates.

Appendices

The Appendices of this resource are designed to provide practical, ready-to-use tools that empower worship leaders, dance and flag ministers, shofar blowers, and staff carriers to minister with biblical insight, creative clarity, and spiritual authority. These are more than resources—they are blueprints for building, equipping, and mobilizing expressive worship teams.

A. Color Symbolism Chart

A Biblical & Prophetic Reference for Use in Flags, Banners, Garments, and Worship Settings

Color	Biblical Symbolism	Scripture References	Prophetic Use in Worship
Red	Redemption, Atonement, Blood of Christ	Exodus 12:13, Hebrews 9:22, Revelation 5:9	Warfare, intercession, salvation-themed worship
Blue	Heaven, Revelation, Authority	Numbers 15:38–39, Exodus 24:10	Divine downloads, prophetic acts, open heavens
White	Purity, Holiness, Victory	Revelation 7:14, Isaiah 1:18, Psalm 51:7	Cleansing, surrender, celebration
Gold	Glory, Kingship, Divinity	Exodus 25:11, Revelation 21:18	God's presence, majesty, high praise moments
Purple	Royalty, Kingship, Priesthood	Esther 8:15, John 19:2, Judges 8:26	Declaring Christ's reign, kingdom identity
Green	New Life, Growth, Healing	Psalm 1:3, Hosea 14:5, Mark 6:39	Healing services, inner restoration
Black	Death to Self, Mystery of God, Authority Over Darkness	Exodus 10:21, Isaiah 45:3, Romans 6:6	Warfare, solemn repentance, overcoming darkness
Silver	Redemption, Refining, Strength	Psalm 66:10, Proverbs 10:20, Malachi 3:3	Surrender, refinement, transition seasons
Orange	Perseverance, Fire, Passion	Daniel 3:25, Acts 2:3	Revival services, pressing through
Yellow	Hope, Joy, Celebration	Psalm 30:5, Isaiah 60:1	Praise, awakening joy, restoration services

B. Types of Shofar Blasts & Their Uses

Blast Name	Hebrew Name	Number of Blasts	Spiritual Meaning	When to Use
Tekiah	תְּקִיעָה	1 long blast	A call to gather, announce God's presence	Start of service, sacred assemblies, call to worship
Shevarim	שְׁבָרִים	3 medium blasts	A broken cry of repentance or intercession	Repentance services, intercession, altar calls
Teruah	תְּרוּעָה	9 short blasts	Warfare, alarm, urgency, wake up call	Spiritual warfare, prayer vigils, night watches
Tekiah Gedolah	תְּקִיעָה גְּדוֹלָה	1 very long blast	Final trumpet, victorious shout, resurrection sound	Closing services, breakthrough declarations

Example Usage for Service:
At the beginning of a prophetic worship night, begin with a Tekiah to call everyone into spiritual attention. During intense intercession, follow with Shevarim to align hearts in repentance. Release Teruah during spiritual warfare songs and end with Tekiah Gedolah to prophetically declare victory.

C. Flag and Dance Team Constitution (Sample)

King's Motion Worship Collective – Ministry Constitution

1. Vision Statement:
To express the heart of God through prophetic movement and visual worship arts that shift atmospheres, bring healing, and glorify Jesus.

2. **Mission Objectives:**
   - ✓ To train dancers and flag bearers in both spiritual and practical excellence
   - ✓ To operate in unity with the worship and pastoral teams
   - ✓ To prophetically minister with honor, modesty, and sensitivity to the Holy Spirit
3. **Team Roles:**
   - ✓ Lead Facilitator: Oversees team, training, and service coordination
   - ✓ Dance Ministers: Express worship through choreographed and spontaneous movement
   - ✓ Flag Bearers: Carry and wave banners in intercession, warfare, and praise
   - ✓ Armor Bearer (Support): Handles garments, props, and care for the team
4. **Core Values:**
   - ✓ Holiness before excellence
   - ✓ Sensitivity to the Spirit over performance
   - ✓ Unity over individualism
   - ✓ Modesty in movement and attire
5. **Ministry Expectations:**
   - ✓ Weekly personal devotion and team prayer
   - ✓ Punctuality for rehearsals and services
   - ✓ Submission to pastoral leadership
   - ✓ Dress modestly (loose, opaque garments) and cover underlayers
   - ✓ Flow with the music and prophetic direction given
6. **Conflict Resolution:**
   - ✓ All issues must be brought first to the team lead, then to pastoral oversight if unresolved. Gossip or divisiveness will not be tolerated.

7. Release Form (Sample):

"I, __________, commit to serve in the King's Motion Worship Collective with integrity, accountability, and submission to the leadership of this house. I understand this is a ministry, not a performance, and I offer my body as a living sacrifice for the glory of God."

(Signed) ________________________

D. Staff Use Manual

Symbolic Use of Staffs in Prophetic Worship

Biblical Foundation:

- ✓ Moses' Rod: Authority, miracles, judgment (Exodus 4:2–5, Exodus 14:16)
- ✓ Aaron's Rod: Confirmation, leadership, priesthood (Numbers 17:8)
- ✓ Jesus as Shepherd: Protection, guidance (Psalm 23:4, John 10:11)

Symbolic Applications:

Gesture	Symbolism	Example Usage
Staff pointed upward	Worship, declaring heaven's reign	"Lift up the rod" moment during a praise break
Staff struck on ground	Authority, alignment, judgment	Prophetic act to break strongholds in intercession
Staff in circular motion	Protection, encircling angels	During healing services, declaring divine protection
Staff laid across shoulders	Yoke bearing, surrender	Used in solemn worship or during deliverance prayers
Staff lifted together in unity	Corporate agreement	All staff carriers raise in one accord during breakthrough song

Materials Needed:

- ✓ Staff: 5–6 feet wooden or lightweight plastic rod
- ✓ Can be wrapped in ribbon (colors per prophetic assignment)
- ✓ Engravings or Scripture decals optional

Training Curriculum Outline:

- ✓ Session 1: Biblical Background of the Rod
- ✓ Session 2: Safe Movements and Symbolic Acts
- ✓ Session 3: Practicing Flow with Music and Team
- ✓ Session 4: Personal Consecration and Anointing Service

Prayer of Commissioning:

"Lord, as I carry this staff, I do not carry wood, but your authority. May this rod be as Moses'—signaling miracles. As Aaron's—signaling leadership. And as yours, Good Shepherd—guiding in love. Use this for your glory."

E. Prophetic Dance & Flag Choreography Chart

This chart serves as a foundational guide for choreographing Spirit-led movement in worship through flags and dance. It includes movement types, color coordination, symbolic meanings, and prophetic applications to create unified, intentional, and Holy Spirit-inspired choreography for ministry settings.

Note:

All movements must flow in unity with the worship

sound and be preceded by prayer and discernment. Flag bearers and dancers should coordinate in rehearsals but remain open to Holy Spirit adjustments in real-time.

Movement/Flag Act	Symbolic Meaning	Color Options	Musical Cue/Timing	Suggested Use
Circular flag sweep (clockwise)	Divine order, release of heavenly flow	Gold, Blue	Transition into spontaneous worship	Create atmosphere of glory
Circular flag sweep (counter)	Breaking cycles, reversing curses	Red, Orange	Intercession or spiritual warfare	During prayer for deliverance
Two dancers mirroring each other	Unity, agreement, covenant	Purple, White	When lyrics declare "We agree," etc.	Healing, unity declarations
Lifting flag high and holding	Exaltation of God, heaven's banner	White, Gold, Royal Blue	High-praise climax	During chorus or key lyric like "We lift You"
Quick flag flicks across air	Sword of Spirit, cutting enemy's lies	Red, Silver	Instrumental section or warfare beat	During breakthrough declarations
Large sweeping arm movement	Washing over congregation with grace/love	Light Blue, White	Slow worship or soaking session	Deliverance or post-sermon healing
Marching steps with flag forward	Taking territory, declaring dominion	Green, Gold	Upbeat rhythm or drumbeat	Jericho-style processions
Flags crossed and uncrossed	Breaking chains, freedom declaration	Red, Purple	Prophetic song or spoken word moment	Deliverance segments
Prophetic spin (1–3 turns)	Holy Spirit whirlwind, breakthrough release	Any vibrant, multicolor	After key lyric on breakthrough	End of song climax or altar call

F. Sample Service Flow with Movement & Sound Integration

This sample outlines how to seamlessly integrate dance, flag, staff, and shofar ministry into a worship service without disrupting the flow of the Spirit or overwhelming the congregation. It maintains order, reverence, and prophetic clarity.

Sample Service Flow: "Encounter Night – Heaven Invades Earth"

1. Pre-Service Atmosphere (15 minutes before start)

- ✓ Flag Bearers: Quiet flag movements around sanctuary (Blue and Gold) to release glory and prepare the space.
- ✓ Dance Intercessor: Walks the aisles slowly with staff, praying silently in tongues—symbolic of establishing the Lord's government.

2. Opening Shofar Blast
   - ✓ Tekiah (Long Blast): Blown from the front of the sanctuary to announce the beginning of the service and invite heavenly attention.
   - ✓ Spoken declaration follows: *"We declare this space belongs to the Lord of Hosts!"*
3. Welcome & Call to Worship (Leader)
   - ✓ Short greeting and opening Scripture (Psalm 24).
   - ✓ Flag Ministry: White and Purple flags lifted in stillness as Psalm is read, signifying purity and royalty.
4. Praise Segment (Upbeat Songs)
   - ✓ Dance team comes forward for choreographed praise set. *Song Example: "Freedom" by Jesus Culture*
   - ✓ Movements: Clapping, stomping, turning, flags in circles of celebration (Red and Yellow for joy and redemption).
5. Transition to Deep Worship (Soaking Song)
   - ✓ Dancers slowly retreat to sides.
   - ✓ Flag Bearers move in silence, using soft Light Blue and White flags for soaking atmosphere.
   - ✓ Shofar: Shevarim Blast during a slow instrumental, aligning with a moment of intercession.
6. Spontaneous Prophetic Flow (Open Moment)
   - ✓ Worship team quiets.

- ✓ Lead Intercessor carries staff to center and declares:
  "As Aaron's rod budded, may dormant promises blossom tonight!"
- ✓ Team follows with quiet prayer movement behind her, releasing fragrance through purple flags (authority, promise).

7. Message / Word
   - ✓ Movements pause.
   - ✓ Worship team transitions into instrumental pad.
   - ✓ All ministry teams sit unless prompted by Spirit.
8. Response & Altar Time
   - ✓ Song: *"Worthy is the Lamb" or prophetic instrumental*
   - ✓ Flag dancers minister personally at the altar—Green (healing) and Red (atonement) waved gently over individuals.
   - ✓ Optional dance piece with cloth streamers to convey surrender.
9. Closing Declaration with Sound

All sound tools used together in finale:

- ✓ Shofar: Tekiah Gedolah
- ✓ Staff raised in unity by male leaders
- ✓ White flags waved overhead by children's team
- ✓ Declaration: *"This territory belongs to Jesus Christ—King of Glory!"*

10. Post-Service Atmosphere
    - ✓ Dancers remain at the altar for ministry.
    - ✓ Flags returned reverently to holders.

Intercessors bless and anoint exits of sanctuary.

About the Author
'GERARD ASSEY'

Gerard Assey is a Graduate in Economics, a PGD in Management (HRD) and holds a Doctorate in Leadership. Gerard holds several International Qualifications in Sales, Debt Collection, Training & Teaching, and is a 'Fellow' of the prestigious 'Institute of Sales & Marketing Management'-UK, a Certified NLP Practitioner, a 'Certified Trainer', an 'Accredited Management Teacher-Behavioral Sciences', a 'Certified Competency Facilitator', a 'Certified Management Consultant'- (the International credentials of a professional management consultant, awarded in accordance with global standards of the ICMCI); and a Certification from the University of Michigan in 'Successful Negotiation: Essential Strategies and Skills'

He is also a Member of the 'National Association of Sales Professionals' backed with several years experience in varied industries, both in India and Overseas. He also holds an 'Etiquette Consultant' Certification from the USA (by Sue Fox, Author of Best Seller: 'Business Etiquette for Dummies'. She has trained some of the top celebrities' world over). He was also a recipient of a scholarship for extensive training in Japan on 'Corporate Management for India'.

Gerard Assey is 'Founder & Chief Corporate Trainer' of the Group: '**Citius, Altius, Fortius Unlimited**'- an organization that **celebrated 20 years of Glorious Service** in 2021, focusing on 3 Core Competencies:

People. Performance. Profit; in functional areas of Sales & Marketing, HR & Organizational Development, covering Recruitment, Training & Consultancy!

Having managed organizations with large Sales Forces in India & Overseas, his specialization cover extensive areas of Sales Training (All levels - Presentation, Negotiation, Key/ Strategic Accounts Management & Managerial Skills for all sectors), Bid Proposal/ Capture Planning/ Management Trainings, Retail Sales, Customer Service & Customer Retention Programs, Training for Prevention & Collection of Debt, Self & Personal Development Programs (Time Management, Teamwork & Team Building, Business Etiquette & Personal Grooming, Leadership & Managerial Skills, People Management Skills, Train-the-Trainer etc), including preparation of Custom-designed Business Manuals for Internal (HR, Induction, and Sales etc) & External use (Instruction, User Manuals).

Gerard has successfully conducted over 6460 Trainings & Workshops (as of June '25) all across India, Middle East, Africa, Europe & S.E. Asia. Besides public programs conducted regularly, both in India & Overseas, he has some of the top names as clients whom he services from Single Owners to large Public & Government undertakings, covering all sectors, for their in-house needs.

His website: www.CollectionSkills.com is the only one in this part of the world to be featured in the 'Collections & Credit Risk Magazine-USA' under 'Who's Who in Training' and ranks TOP, along with other websites listed below on most search engines.

Gerard is author of 198 books already (July 2025), all the books being available on all online platforms and outlets as E-books and Paperbacks

A few of our business related books:

1. Bite-sized Bits on Commonsense Management
2. Heart to Heart on Life's Principles'
3. How to become a Successful Manager
4. The Sales Professionals' Master Workbook of S.Y.S.T.E.M.S
5. The Professional Business Email Etiquette Handbook & Guide
6. The Professional Business Video-Conferencing Etiquette Handbook & Guide
7. Professional Presentation Skills
8. Exceptional Customer Service
9. Professional Tele-Marketing Skills
10. Professional Debt Collection Skills
11. The G.R.E.A.T. Sales & Service Workbook
12. Sales Training Advantage for Results (*The Ultimate Sales Training Manual to enable you stand out as a S.T.A.R.*)
13. CEO Daily Planner & Organizer
14. The Sales Professionals' Master Daily Planner
15. The Professional Debt Collector's Master Daily Planner
16. My Daily Planner & Organizer
17. MY EMERGENCY INFORMATION RECORD (Family Emergency & Peace of Mind Planner)
18. The Ultimate Therapist & Counselors Planner and Organizer
19. Building an Ethical Workplace
20. Managing Relationships at Work
21. Managing Business Meetings Effectively
22. Effective Delegation Skills
23. Goal Setting for Success
24. B2B Selling by Email
25. Professional Business Etiquette & Grooming
26. Dining Etiquette & Table Manners
27. Effective Networking Skills
28. Grooming, Etiquette & Manners for Teens, Young Adults & Future Leaders
29. Inter-Personal Skills
30. Get Ready, Get Hired!
31. Selling in a Recession
32. Effective Receivables Management in an Economic Downturn!
33. Real Estate & Property Sales Training
34. Credit Sales & Accounts Receivable Management

35. Selling Skills for Real Estate & Property Advisors
36. Take G.R.E.A.T. C.A.R.E!
37. Spa, Salon & Health Club Selling Skills
38. Selling Travel, Holiday & MICE Services
39. Selling Skills for Spa's, Salons & Health Clubs
40. Retailing in Salons & Spas
41. Selling Holiday, Vacation, Tours & Packages
42. The Power of Sales Referrals
43. Selling Luxury
44. Technical Selling Skills
45. Financial Advisors Sales Training
46. Dealing with Burnout at Work Monopolize Your Markets
47. Selling to Affluent Customers
48. Growing up with Grace
49. Financial Selling Skills
50. *The Effective Manager's Guide: Key Skills to Thrive*
51. From Aspiring to Inspiring: A Guide for New Managers on the Rise
52. The Power of Focus
53. Selling with Integrity: Sell Like Jesus The Perfect Role Model!
54. 31 Habits of Champions: Your 31-Day Journey to Greatness
55. Rejecting Grasshopper Talk: From Grasshopper to Giant-Killer-*Defeating Giants Daily!*
56. Navigate the AI-Powered Future of Bid & Proposals: Up-Skill to Stay Relevant with Alternative Career Paths & Opportunities
57. Hiring Sales Winners
58. Present with Impact
59. Success Unlocked: *Breaking Free from Habits that Hold You Back*
60. Complaints to Cheers, Feedback to Gold: Mastering Complaints Management
61. Thriving Together: *Cultivating Diversity, Equity, and Inclusion*
62. Coaching Skills for Sales Managers
63. Soaring to Success in Business & Leadership: Swifter, Higher, Stronger!
64. From Classroom to Podium: A Student's Guide to Powerful Public Speaking & Presentation Skills
65. Developing Self-Discipline
66. The CEO's 31-Day Power Plan: Unlocking Success through Essential Traits

67. Credibility Matters
68. A Winning Attitude
69. Bid & Proposal Management Using AI
70. Sales Forecasting: A Practical & Proven Guide to Strategic Sales Forecasting
71. Elevate & Energize: *50 Dynamic & Fun Activities for Peak Workplace Morale*
72. 'Sales SOS! Sales on Fire! *30 Days to Conquer Chaos & the Nightmares of Success!'*
73. Mastering Sales Managerial Skills: *Building High-Performing Teams & Driving Exceptional Results*
74. Eagle-Eyed Leadership: Unleashing the Power of 31 Lessons from Eagles
75. The Ultimate Employee Training Guide: *Training Today, Leading Tomorrow*
76. Being More Accountable at Work
77. Creating a Culture of Continuous Improvement
78. Effective Questioning & Listening Skills
79. The Power of Value Selling
80. The Growth Mindset
81. Mastering Professional Help Desk Skills
82. The Power to Lead with Empathy
83. Being Prepared: The Key to Unlocking Success
84. Youthful Spark-Youth Energizers, Activities and Games-Igniting the Fun in Youth
85. Ignite your Motivation for Success
86. Elevate Your Executive Presence: *Your Roadmap to Executive Excellence*
87. Smart Decisions: *Mastering Problem Solving with Strategic Solutions for Business Success*
88. Strategic Planning: *Developing and Implementing Strategic Plans to Achieve Long-Term Business Goals*
89. The Power of Stay Interviews
90. Developing G.R.I.T.
91. Adaptability
92. Diagnosis- *A Key Skill for Leadership*
93. The Burnout-Proof Salesperson: *The Master Guide to Preventing Stress & Burnout-* Strategies for Thriving in Sales
94. Learning from Failure: *Keys to Success*
95. Customer Success Management
96. Overcoming the Killers of Motivation
97. The C-Suite Code: *Mastering Skills for Executive Excellence'*

98. Dealing with Difficult Customers
99. Unlocking Your Potential: Mastering the Top 20 Life Skills for a Brighter Future
100. Nurturing Tomorrow's Leaders: *Essential Soft Skills Every Child Must Learn*
101. Lively & Fun Party Games for Seniors & Elders
102. Role Playing for Sales Champions: From Practice to Performance
103. Fun and Exciting Party Games for Kids
104. Case Studies for Sales
105. Role-Playing for Unbeatable Customer Service
106. Case Studies in Customer Service
107. Case Studies in Winning Negotiations
108. Case Studies in Management & Leadership
109. Case Studies in Human Resources & Talent Management
110. CEO Success Blueprint: The Essential Toolkit for CEOs and C-Level Executives
111. The Salesperson's Self-Coaching Guide: *Master Your Own Self-Coaching Plan for Success*
112. Overcoming Procrastination: *Your Ultimate Guide to Stop Delaying and Start Living Your Best Life*
113. When True Colors Are Exposed: *The Journey to Unmasking Humanity*
114. Life-Changing Habits for Teens: Teen Success Blueprint for a Bright Future
115. Workplace Stress-Free: *Proven Strategies to Thrive at Work and Beyond*
116. Objection Overruled: *The Ultimate Guide to Turning 'No' into 'Yes'*
117. Building Strong Teams: *A Comprehensive Guide to Team Building*
118. Ethical & Moral Leadership in Business: *Eliminating Unethical Practices & Building a Culture of Trust & Integrity*
119. Rising Strong: Building Positive: High Self-Esteem for a Fulfilling Life-*A Practical Guide for Students, Employees, Leaders & Entrepreneurs*

From the Ministry side, Gerard graduated in the very first batch of Charis Bible College-India & had for over 9 years served as a Part-time Faculty at Charis Bible College-Chennai (Andrew Wommack Ministries-Colorado, USA).

He also holds a Diploma in Worship (a subject closest to his heart) from the JSOW and is also a graduate of the Advanced Mentorship Program (AMP) and the Circle Of Ministerial Engagement (C.O.M.E.) of Prophet Jerome Fernando and a Spiritual Son of the Esteemed Prophet.

An accomplished author of several Secular & Christian Books, Gerard has been on the board of a few international organizations and boasts of being the SON of the MOST HIGH GOD: An ordinary guy following an extraordinary GOD!

...And some of his most recent Christian Books being:

1. A Bouquet of Praises for My KING
2. Christian Jokes for the Serious Religious' Folks!
3. Jesus Healed You!
4. Praise24Ever! (also in Tamil version)
5. The 5G Network of GOD
6. Building Faith over F.E.A.R- FACE EVERYTHING AND RISE with JESUS
7. Hebrew and Greek Praise and Worship Words
8. Godly Mothers' and Grandmothers' Bible Story time for Kids!
9. Miracles of Jesus in Pictures
10. Raise your Praise all 365 Days
11. Thanking GOD with an Attitude of Gratitude
12. Meditating on the Attributes of GOD
13. Puppet Scripts
14. Alcohol Ruins, JESUS Reforms, Renews & Restores!
15. Habakkuk 2:2 Christian Daily Journal, Planner & Organizer
16. ABC of GOD's Word for Handwriting Practice
17. Daily Bible Verse Handwriting Practice (Building Godly Character & Faith through Cursive Handwriting Practice!)
18. Guiding Light: Fun & Faith-Building Bible Activities for Children
19. Rejecting Grasshopper Talk: From Grasshopper to Giant-Killer-*Defeating Giants Daily!*
20. Teen Titans of Faith: *Building Courage, Determination & Christ-like-Esteem*
21. I AM Empowered: *Unleashing Divine Power with Positive Declarations*
22. Be A Solution Provider-*From Passion to Purpose: A Biblical Guide to Being the Answer to the World!*
23. Miracles of JESUS
24. Parables of Jesus for a Meaningful Life!
25. A Grateful Heart: Importance of Sharing Testimonies of GOD's Grace

26. Melodies of Worship to JESUS: 31 Songs of Praise & Worship From My Heart to HIS!
27. I AM SO BLESSED!
28. My Daily Cup of Energizer
29. 31 Leadership Lessons *from* Jesus- *The Supreme Leader*
30. Peace Amidst Storms: A Biblical Guide to Conquering S.T.R.E.S.S.
31. Rise Above: 20 Biblical Eagle Lessons for Life's Triumphs
32. Godly Goal Setting: *The FAITHFUL Blueprint for a Purpose-Driven Life*
33. The Profound Attributes of our Mighty GOD: Understanding the 10S's of the Almighty
34. Worship Now, Worship Forever: *A Journey from Earthly Praise to Eternal Glory*
35. Unceasing Praise & Worship: *365 Days to Worship the King*
36. The ROAR Within: *Living with Purpose and Authority through the Power of the Holy Spirit*
37. From Potential to Purpose: Unlocking and Multiplying Your Talents & Gifts for Kingdom Impact
38. Songs from the Heart: *Worshipping GOD in Your Own Tune & Melody*
39. Awakening Praise & Worship: Hebrew & Greek Words to Raise Your Praise
40. Sing a NEW Song to the LORD Everyday: *Daily Devotions of Praise & Worship to Lift Your Heart & Glorify HIS Name*
41. *The* A.R.O.M.A. of True Worship: *Creating Worship That Delights God*
42. Becoming A Kingdom Champion: *Embracing God's Call for a Life of Purpose & Victory*
43. The Busy Businessman's Daily Devotional: 366 Crisp Truths to Start Your Day Strong
44. The Teacher's Heart: *Daily Devotions for Educators*
45. Anchored! *A 31-Day Devotional for Students Facing Life's Challenges*
46. Suddenly! Unlocking Unorthodox Breakthroughs through Unusual Worship
47. Overcoming Adversity: *Lessons from the Bible for Modern Challenges*
48. LORD, Don't do it without me
49. Kingdom Leadership: *Biblical Principles for Modern Leaders*
50. Heartprints of God- *Growing God's Way:* Daily Devotions for Kids to Shine Bright
51. Send Judah First: Let your Praises Go up First to See the

Mighty Move of GOD

52. DIVINE MOMENTS: *Recognizing, Embracing, Preparing, and Walking into Life-Changing Encounters with God*
53. Be a Builder in the Kingdom: *The C.E.M.E.N.T. Guide to Creating a Lasting Legacy*
54. Unshakable: *Pillars of Godly Womanhood* (Pillars of Faith That Changed History)
55. Lead Like a Shepherd: *14 Essential Traits for Pastoral Excellence*
56. The Worship Leader's Arsenal: *Powerful Exhortations to Ignite Thanksgiving, Praise & Worship*
57. Women of UnShakable Faith: *31-Day Devotional for Strength, Purpose & Influence*
58. Called to Teach: *A Complete 10-Week Training Guide for Impactful VBS Teachers*
59. Strumming for the KING: Cowboy Songs of Faith & Fire
60. The Ultimate Youth Camp Playbook: *50 Bible-Centered Indoor Games to Engage, Equip, and Empower Teens*
61. Glad in HIS Presence: *David's Revelation of GOD's Love & Mercy*
62. The Spirit Behind the Sound: *52 Devotionals for Worship Teams*
63. THE COWBOY'S COMPASS: *Riding the Trail of Faith with Grit & Grace*
64. Worship as My Weapon: *Living Victoriously through the Power of Praise*
65. A Worshipper Always Wins*: Living a Life of Victorious Worship*
66. Worship That Leads to the Throne: *Practical Strategies for Worship Leaders to Inspire Their Team & Usher People into God's Presence*
67. Worship as Warfare: *Conquering through the Sound of Surrender*
68. Watchmen on the Walls: *A 31-Day Devotional for Worship Teams*
69. KINGDOM BUSINESS: *52 Biblical Principles for GODLY Leadership & Wise Decisions*
70. From Evening to Morning: *Rediscovering GOD's Sacred Hours*
71. Waves of Glory: *Worship through Dance, Flags, Staff & Sound*

Besides regularly contributing to business & trade journals, including international ones such as the 'Creative Training Techniques' and the 'Sales News' of the U.S.A, He is also a member of several prestigious bodies & trade associations, having participated in many Conferences & Workshops in India & Overseas.

Prior to his last assignment of leading & managing a large MNC as head, Gerard had a 3-year stint in the Middle East as a Consultant with a leading British Consultancy Firm.

As the past 'Official Country Representative' for the International Business Award- 'THE STEVIES'-(the business world's own Oscar) for about 4 years- he ensured a few Indian companies that qualify for the same every year!

Gerard can be contacted at:
Email: training@Sales-Training.in,training@CollectionSkills.com
Websites:

www.Sales-Training.in
www.EtiquetteWorks.in
www.CollectionSkills.com
www.RetailSalesTraining.in
www.SalesTrainingIndia.com
www.ManualPreparation.com
www.TrainingWithPuppets.com
www.FirstContactAcademy.com
www.SalesAndMarketingRecruiter.com

www.ingramcontent.com/pod-product-compliance
Ingram Content Group UK Ltd.
Pitfield, Milton Keynes, MK11 3LW, UK
UKHW021340190726
13845UKWH00027B/645